THE
BEAST
or
THE
LAMB

THE
BEAST
or
THE
LAMB

DISCERNING THE
NATURE THAT
DETERMINES YOUR DESTINY

DEREK PRINCE

Chosen

a division of Baker Publishing Group
Minneapolis, Minnesota

Published by Chosen Books
11400 Hampshire Avenue South
Minneapolis, Minnesota 55438
www.chosenbooks.com

Chosen Books is a division of
Baker Publishing Group, Grand Rapids, Michigan

Printed in the United States of America

ISBN 978-0-8007-6253-7 (trade paper)
ISBN 978-0-8007-6278-0 (casebound)
ISBN 978-1-4934-3719-1 (ebook)
Library of Congress Control Number: 2022006102

Cover design by Rob Williams, InsideOut Creative Arts, Inc.

Baker Publishing Group publications use paper produced from sustainable forestry practices and post-consumer waste whenever possible.

22 23 24 25 26 27 28   7 6 5 4 3 2 1

Publisher's Note

This book was compiled from the extensive archive of Derek Prince's unpublished materials and approved by the Derek Prince Ministries International editorial team.

CONTENTS

———————— PART 3 ————————

CHOOSING THE LAMB, EMPOWERED BY THE DOVE   147

INTRODUCTION

Does it seem strange at first sight to have two animals mentioned in the same title or sentence? Does that combination pique your interest and kindle a desire to find out more?

In essence, this book is about the contrasting characters of the wild Beast and the Lamb as revealed in Scripture—the false christ and the true Christ. The Beast and the Lamb represent two completely opposite natures. The wild Beast is cunning, deceitful, arrogant, boastful, vicious, cruel, treacherous, murderous, despotic and dominating. In contrast, the Lamb is truthful, peaceable, humble, meek, pure, strong, simple and self-sacrificial.

The Bible reveals that Satan is behind the Beast, while Jesus Christ is the Lamb of God who takes away the sin of the world. A third creature we will discuss in some detail is the Dove—which represents the Holy Spirit. (Later in this book, we will learn more about this key note: The Holy Spirit will only rest and remain on the nature of the Lamb.)

You and I have a choice before us. We will either choose to cultivate the nature of the Lamb or the nature of the Beast. Unfortunately, most believers have never been taught how to discern the difference between these two natures. Nor have most of us realized that, by our thoughts and actions, we are presently assuming one nature or the other. Of even greater significance, we have not been informed that this intrinsic choice will actually determine our ultimate destiny in life.

Unapologetically, this book represents a very significant and important part of God's total revelation concerning the end times. I believe that Christians who do not take the trouble to find out the basic teaching of the Word of God about the Antichrist and the spirit of Antichrist are in great danger of being swept away by deception.

For our protection and enlightenment, God has made knowledge available to us—and we are responsible to find it and decide what we should do with it.

This is not an easy study. To get the most out of it, you will need to use your mind to comprehend and follow the revelation of Scripture. Let's trust God together to give us understanding and insight.

We will examine a great deal of content in this book. Here is my advice and encouragement: Do not try to read through it too quickly. Take time to let these truths soak in. Otherwise, as with a hard rain on dry ground, there may be runoff, and you may not receive the refreshing rain you need. If you will allow yourself to be immersed in this content about the Beast, the Lamb (and the Dove), availing yourself of the Word and the Spirit, you will be able to absorb these truths to the fullest extent.

Much has been written about the end times—some of it by me. But I believe that if you allow this message to penetrate deep into your heart, it will not only prepare you to live an effective, empowered life here on earth in the challenging days ahead, it will also prepare you for a glorious eternity in the presence of the Lamb.

PART 1

—

UNDERSTANDING the NATURE of the WILD BEAST

Very often in life, it is necessary for us to look at the negative to fully appreciate the positive. How can we be thankful for warmth if we have never been cold? How can we appreciate springtime if we have not survived the winter? How can we savor the day unless we have endured the night?

In the spiritual dimension, you and I can take this principle even deeper by asking ourselves: Can I truly appreciate the life Jesus bought for me on the cross if I have not followed Him through death, burial and resurrection?

In seeking to understand and appreciate the glory, the power and the wonder of the Lamb of God, Jesus Christ, it is necessary to start by looking at His—and our—greatest opponent: Satan. In the first part of this book, we will examine some of what Scripture reveals about Satan, the Beast and the Antichrist.

1

Many Antichrists

What do we mean by "antichrist"? It is important for us first to know the meaning of the word itself. The word "Christ" is taken from the Greek word *Christos*, which corresponds to the Hebrew word *Meshiach*, or in English, "Messiah." It means "the Anointed One."

When we speak about Jesus Christ, we are speaking about Jesus the Messiah. Thus the Antichrist is someone who is the anti-Messiah.

The Double Meaning of "Anti"

The preposition *anti* in front of *christ* or *messiah* has two meanings, both of which apply to the Antichrist's activities. First of all, *anti* means "against" or "opposing." Of course, we use that regularly in modern speech, for example in the terms *antibacterial* or *antisocial*. But the other meaning is less well understood. It means "in place of."

We can understand the operation of the Antichrist as having two phases:

1. To come *against* the true Christ to get Him out of the way, and
2. To *replace* Him with a false christ.

Three Forms of Antichrist

In 1 John 2:18, John speaks about the connection between the Antichrist and the last days. He says:

> Little children, it is the last hour [not just the last day, mind you, but the last hour]; and as you have heard that the Antichrist is coming, even now many antichrists have come, by which we know that it is the last hour.

Seeing evidences of the activity of the spirit of the Antichrist is a distinctive mark of the end times.

Then in 1 John 4:2 we read: "By this you know the Spirit of God [the Holy Spirit]: Every spirit that confesses that Jesus Christ has come in the flesh is of God."

That is, every spirit that confesses that Jesus came in human form and lived as man with flesh and blood is of God.

Verse 3 completes the thought:

> Every spirit that does not confess that Jesus Christ has come in the flesh is not of God. And this is the spirit of the Antichrist, which you have heard was coming, and is now already in the world.

Within the verses we have cited above, we see three forms of "antichrist":

14

1. *many* antichrists, plural
2. *the* Antichrist, singular
3. the *spirit* of the Antichrist—the spirit of antichrist which operates through *every* antichrist.

This last truth is a supremely important concept to grasp: *Any antichrist is controlled by the spirit of the Antichrist.* Throughout history, there have been many antichrists who have arisen. The Jewish Encyclopedia records at least forty false messiahs who have come to the Jewish people since the time of Jesus. They were all antichrists.

Probably the most famous example was Simon Bar Kochba. He led a revolt against Rome from around AD 132 to 135. Then in the fifth century came Moses of Crete. He persuaded people that they should wade out into the sea from Crete in order to meet the Messiah. Thousands of his followers went into the sea and were drowned. In the year 1666 (which was supposed to be a miraculous year), Sabbatai Zevi claimed to be the Messiah, and he was enthusiastically received by multitudes.

The history of Europe also records many antichrists. Down through the ages in the history of the Church there have been ungodly men who claimed to be ministers of Christ and who led immoral and dissonant lives.

If we look to the Middle East, one outstanding antichrist is Mohammed. (We will deal more with Mohammed and the religion of Islam in a later chapter when we look at examples of the spirit of the Antichrist.)

In Zaire (now the Democratic Republic of the Congo) in central Africa, there was an African religious leader who declared straight-out that he was Jesus. But then he died. Very wisely, the political leadership in Zaire would not allow the people to bury his body. They set a guard around it, and then after three days, they let the people take the body away and bury it. Not surprisingly, the Africans who had believed him got very angry, and they threw stones at the coffin because they realized they had been deceived by this false messiah.

In the history of many nations of the earth, you will find the record of many antichrists. What makes them antichrist is *the spirit of the Antichrist*—the spiritual force that works in them and for them.

To Modern Times

Interestingly, just to bring this subject closer to the present, in the summer of 1988 in Jerusalem, elegant posters were circulated on all the main streets of the city. They read in Hebrew: "Messiah has come and if you want to meet Him, go to the Mount of Olives on [a certain Sunday] and He will be there."

I have no idea who printed the posters, but they were beautifully done. I know of one journalist who went to the Mount of Olives to see what might happen, but he did not find the Messiah. I relate this story to show how real this issue is. People are looking for the Messiah. If you talk to Jewish people in a sympathetic attitude and you use the name *Messiah*, something changes in their eyes. It is a word that has a special significance for Jewish people.

Down through the pages of history from the time of John's writings until the modern day, there have been *many* antichrists. However, there is one who is called *the* Antichrist who has not yet appeared on the stage of human history. He is the ultimate manifestation of the spirit of the Antichrist. I am inclined to believe that his coming is so near that we might say his shadow has already fallen across the stage of history. That, however, is just my personal opinion.

As we progress through this book, particularly in Part 1: Understanding the Nature of the Wild Beast, I would encourage you to keep asking yourself the following questions as you consider this material:

1. Does this refer to the spirit of the Antichrist?
2. Does it refer to one of the many antichrists?
3. Does it refer to *the* Antichrist?

This questioning exercise will be a part of the discernment process you and I need to develop as we learn to navigate this important subject.

In the next chapter, we will look at four specific marks that Scripture tells us are likely to be manifest where the spirit of the Antichrist is in operation.

2

MARKS OF THE SPIRIT
OF ANTICHRIST

Having seen that there are three manifestations of the spirit of the Antichrist, along with specific examples of some of the many antichrists, it is imperative that we can identify the marks of the spirit of the Antichrist. We must understand the ways to discern this spirit. Thankfully, they are clearly provided for us in Scripture.

The First Mark—It Goes Out from Us

We see the first mark in 1 John 2:19:

> [Many antichrists] went out from us, but they were not of us; for if they had been of us, they would have continued with us; but they went out that they might be made manifest, that none of them were of us.

This is a very important point for us to recognize: The spirit of the Antichrist *begins in association with the people of God.* It is amazing to see that the spirit of the Antichrist is never totally removed from Scripture. It is *not* paganism. It always arises in clear view of the fact that Jesus has come. By way of a denial, it is always related to the true Christ. Here is the most important part of this truth: Those who adhere to the Antichrist do not remain with Christians; they go out from Christianity.

This is significant because it indicates, if I understand it rightly, that the Antichrist will arise somehow in association with professing Christians. In other words, he is not going to be some dictator who has no Christian profession or association. Rather, he will be closely associated with the professing Church.

I do not believe we will see the spirit of the Antichrist operating in areas of this earth where the Gospel has never been preached. The spirit of the Antichrist will only operate where the true Christ has first been presented.

When Satan was bargaining with Jesus about the kingdoms of this world (recorded in Matthew 4, Mark 1 and Luke 4), Jesus said to Satan, "Get behind Me, Satan!" However, that is not really a correct translation. What Jesus said was, "Follow behind Me, Satan." In other words, "I will go first, and you can come after."

Everywhere the true Christ has been preached, we can expect the spirit of the Antichrist to manifest itself in due course. It cannot be manifested where the true Christ has not been preached because it has no relevance, for it is essentially a denial that Jesus is the Christ. If no one has preached Jesus—if no one has preached the true Christ in a way that produces true believers—then the spirit of the Antichrist has nothing to work upon. The emergence of the Antichrist is Satan's retaliation, or counterattack, against the Gospel of the Kingdom and its King, Jesus Christ.

The Second Mark—It Denies the Father-Son Relationship

Continuing with the passage we just cited, in verses 22–23 of 1 John 2, we see this question:

> Who is a liar but he who denies that Jesus is the Christ [the Messiah]? He is antichrist who denies the Father and the Son. Whoever denies the Son does not have the Father either; he who acknowledges the Son has the Father also.

This passage gives us another mark of the spirit of the Antichrist: *It denies the relationship of the Father and the Son* within the Godhead. It does not acknowledge this revelation of our unique God.

I will deal with this subject more specifically in the next chapter, but as I mentioned before, this repudiation of the Father-Son relationship is very conspicuous in one of the most powerful anti-Christian forces in the world—Islam, the religion of Mohammed. This religion ferociously denies that Jesus is the Son of God. It will acknowledge that Jesus may have been the Messiah—but *not* the Son of God. The great mosque of Omar, which stands on the temple site in Jerusalem, has inscriptions in Arabic all around its dome. Twice the words state emphatically, "God has no need of a son."

Years ago, I was praying with a Muslim who wanted salvation, and I said, "Let me lead you in a prayer." When I said, "Jesus, the Son of God," his mouth shut like a trap. He would not say it.

In 1985, my wife, Ruth, and I were ministering in the nation of Pakistan. Because we had announced our intention to pray for healing in these meetings, thousands of people had come, even though it was a Muslim state. During the meetings, we estimated that eight or nine thousand people had indicated they wanted to be saved. I would always lead them in a prayer, asking them to repeat after me. (The results of how many actually prayed the prayer are known only to God.) But I would always start my prayer this way: "Lord Jesus Christ, I believe You are the Son of God and the only way to God." Why did I pray in that way? Because any spiritual authority or force that denies the relationship of the Son and the Father in the Godhead is an antichrist mark, and I needed to counteract that deception with the truth.

My personal impression is that Islam is probably the most active, powerful anti-Christian force at work in the world at the present time. Unfortunately, multitudes of Christians are deceived about this fact, because they have not learned to discern the marks we are talking about in this book.

The Third Mark—It Denies that Jesus Came in the Flesh

A third mark of the spirit of the Antichrist is found in 1 John 4:1–2:

> Beloved, do not believe every spirit, but test the spirits, whether they are of God; because many false prophets have gone out into the world. By this you know the Spirit of God: Every spirit that confesses that Jesus Christ has come in the flesh is of God.

This spirit we are investigating denies that Jesus has come in the flesh. The truth that the Messiah came as a man of flesh and blood is a fact that the spirit of the Antichrist will not affirm.

This is one supreme test of what kind of spirit you are dealing with. Whether you are actually dealing with a demon in a person or a doctrine someone espouses, if you do not find a clear willingness to acknowledge that Jesus the Messiah has come in the flesh, you can know that the underlying spirit is not from God.

The Fourth Mark—It Does Not Confess Jesus

For the fourth mark, we refer to 1 John 4:3—

> Every spirit that does not confess that Jesus Christ has come in the flesh is not of God. And this is the spirit of the Antichrist, which you have heard was coming, and is now already in the world.

This more general mark is related to the previous one but is slightly different. To make this general point, we are leaving out the part about Him coming in the flesh, as we have dealt with that already. The word "confess" is derived from a Latin word that means "to say the same as," and it comes from the translation of the Greek word that means "to say the same as." So confession is saying the same as. Saying the same as what? The answer is saying the same as God has already said in His Word. Or, to say it another way, it is making the words of your mouth agree with the written Word of God. Unequivocally, we can say that any spirit that does not acknowledge what the Bible says about Jesus is an antichrist spirit.

Can you understand then that the spirit of the Antichrist is not paganism? Do you see that it can only arise in a place where the claims of Jesus have been stated already? This spirit of the Antichrist is Satan's ultimate counterattack against Jesus and against the Gospel.

The First Manifestation of the Spirit of the Antichrist

My personal impression is that the Bible actually records the first time the spirit of the Antichrist really manifested itself—namely in Matthew 27:21–22, where Jesus stood before Pilate and the Jewish religious leaders were accusing Him. You probably will remember that the issue to be decided was whether Jesus or Barabbas should be released. Pilate intended to release one prisoner. Which would they choose?

> The governor answered and said to them, "Which of the two do you want me to release to you?"
> They said, "Barabbas!"
> Pilate said to them, "What then shall I do with Jesus who is called Christ [or Messiah]?" They all said to him, "Let Him be crucified!"

It seems obvious that this was a deliberate rejection of Jesus and a choosing of another in His place. The one who was chosen, Barabbas, was a political figure and a man of violence—a murderer. This unexpected choice by the crowd is one of the most amazing facts of human history. Clearly, the Jewish crowd was rejecting Jesus and choosing Barabbas, even though Jesus had done nothing but good. He had never harmed anyone. He had healed countless people—some of whom may have been in the crowd—and He had brought peace and love to multitudes.

Why did the Jews make that tragic mistake? My answer would be that, without understanding it, they were overwhelmed by a spirit—the spirit of the Antichrist.

I am not saying this in order to be accusatory or condemning. Let us not point our fingers at them. In fact, when the time comes for us to make such a choice, we should be very careful not to make the same mistake ourselves.

A spiritual force swept through that crowd and it changed them. They became almost insane with anger, jealousy and rage, without any justifiable cause. I believe that is the moment when the spirit of the Antichrist first appeared on the stage of humanity. In many ways, that spirit has sought to dominate the Jewish people from that time until now.

A Terrible Lesson

Have you noticed that God never teaches in theory only? We may say, "Lord, I really learned that principle." But God's reply will be: "Fine. Now let's see it worked out in your life." The same test that faced the Jewish people that day will also face the rest of humanity, and the people of earth are going to get the most terrible lesson they have ever had.

Pontius Pilate brought before the Jewish people two men, Jesus and Barabbas, giving them a choice between a violent criminal and Jesus. At the end of this age, the human race will make a similar choice. They will say, "We don't want this Christ. Instead, give us the leader of our choice. Give us this brilliant, talented, supernaturally empowered man. We want *him.*"

In the case of Jesus and Barabbas, the Jewish people got what they asked for. The chief priests had said to Pilate, "We have no king but Caesar!" (John 19:15), which was an amazing statement for Jews to make. Now for nineteen centuries, they have been ruled by "the Caesars," and the Barabbas-types have been turned loose upon them over and over.

While these sad facts are the essence of Jewish history, a similar sequence of events is going to happen to the human race. We are going to get what we choose. Those who choose Jesus will be under His government. Those who reject Jesus will be under the government of the Antichrist.

Jesus had warned the Jewish people about this when they were disputing His claim to be the Messiah, the Son of God: "I have come in My Father's name, and you do not receive Me; if another comes in his own name, him you will receive" (John 5:43). Unfortunately, that warning has proved abundantly true. He is the true Messiah, but people choose false messiahs instead.

I believe this warning from Jesus is a preview of what is going to happen in the world, when God will confront the human race with a choice: Do you want Jesus, or do you want someone else? The same spiritual force that motivated the crowd in Jesus' day will cause the vast majority of people to declare, "Away with Jesus, we'll choose . . ." Whomever they choose will be infinitely worse than Barabbas.

I believe that it is vital to instruct Christians about this, so that we will not make the wrong choice or follow a crowd that is going after the Antichrist.

3

HISTORICAL EXAMPLES OF THE SPIRIT OF ANTICHRIST

The truth is liable to be controversial. While I have no desire to offend anybody, nor do I have any reason to attack other religions, some people may find objectionable the following overview of some of the long-standing, historical examples of the spirit of the Antichrist in operation.

Judaism

The first and most persistent manifestation of the spirit of the Antichrist can be found in Judaism. Now when I say *Judaism*, I am chiefly referring to Orthodox Judaism.

Traditional thinking portrays Christianity as having branched off from Judaism, and that is what the Jewish people will basically tell you has happened. I am not Jewish (although my wife is), and we are very, very close to the Jewish people. And I would say that true Christianity (that is, following the teaching of Jesus and His disciples, not "churchianity") is, in fact, the true continuation of the religion of the Old Testament. By that token, Judaism has deviated from the true way and branched off from it.

Paul described this: "You will say then, 'Branches were broken off that I might be grafted in'" (Romans 11:19). They fell, they were unbelieving and we may say, "Here am I; I am a believer, and I am in the tree." According to Paul, that is true:

> Well said. Because of unbelief they were broken off, and you stand by faith. Do not be haughty, but fear. For if God did not spare the natural branches, He may not spare you either. Therefore consider the goodness and severity of God: on those who fell, severity; but toward you, goodness, if you continue in His goodness. Otherwise you also will be cut off.
>
> Romans 11:20–22

If you bear no fruit, you forfeit the Kingdom (see Matthew 21:43). Israel forfeited the Kingdom because they did not bring forth the fruit. Any group on earth that does not bring forth fruit will forfeit the Kingdom.

Let's take a look at some of the marks of the influence of antichrist, as outlined earlier: Immediately, we can recognize the first mark: Judaism started in association with the people of God. Even a cursory analysis of its teaching reveals an unacknowledged refusal to believe in Jesus. Much of what is taught in Judaism either tacitly or overtly denies the claims of Jesus.

The second manifestation of antichrist in Judaism is, of course, very straightforward. It denies the Father-Son relationship within the Godhead. It rejects the claim of Jesus to be the Son of God and does not accept that God has a Son.

Third, as I have said, it denies that Messiah has come in the flesh. And fourth, Judaism denies that Jesus is the Messiah as revealed in Scripture. Even though Jews strongly believe in a Messiah who is to come, they do not confess that Jesus is the Messiah.

A Jewish friend of mine who had become a believer began talking to his neighbors about his newfound faith. Soon afterward, he received a visit from the local rabbi, who said to him, "I hope you won't talk to anybody about what you believe." My friend answered, "Well, I feel absolutely free to share my faith with those who are interested. I'm not ashamed, and I'm not afraid."

The rabbi said to him, "I would rather that people became anything—Marxists, atheists, it doesn't matter what—anything other than believing what you believe." Do you see that for what it is? That kind of position (neither reasonable nor logical) reveals the spirit of the Antichrist.

Islam

Mohammed came to prominence in the Arabian Peninsula in the seventh century, and he considered himself to be a prophet. He claimed to have received from an archangel the revelation of the religion that then became Islam. He further claimed that his religion, Islam, was the true fulfillment of the Old and the New Testaments; he proposed that the Christians and the gospels had perverted the real truth, but that he, through Islam, was restoring it.

At first, he believed that because he had rejected idolatry and the claims of Christianity, the Jewish people would follow him. But he was disappointed. When they did not follow him, he turned against them as well, becoming a persecutor of the Jewish people.

Wherever Islam gains power and dominance, it will first and foremost suppress the Jews and secondly suppress the Christians. You may be familiar with the statement radical Muslims make: that they will first destroy the "Saturday People" (the Jews, who observe the Sabbath on a Saturday) and then the "Sunday People" (the Christians, who traditionally observe Sunday as a day of rest).

Throughout the centuries, Christians and Jews in Muslim countries have been given the title *dimmy*—which means "second-class people." It seems to suit Islam to have some of these second-class people around, but to keep them in such a low and debased condition that the superiority of Islam becomes evident to everybody.

When Ruth and I were in Pakistan in 1985, one of the first places we were taken to visit was the Christian community in Karachi. I still remember the awful experience of nausea when I saw the squalor, the poverty and the debased conditions in which they lived. Open sewers ran in the streets, and people relieved themselves out in the open.

This Pakistani version of Christianity is just one of many examples of how both Christians and Jews have been forced into the position of a suppressed, inferior minority in Islamic countries. Another example: In the judicial system, the oath of a Christian is not accepted in the courts. The evidence of a Christian against a Muslim is never accepted.

Admittedly, Islam has not been guilty of anything so terrible as the Holocaust of the Second World War. But it has a long record over thirteen centuries of suppression and contempt for Christianity. In fact, the Judeo-Christian traits that have long been regarded as admirable in Western society, such as mercy, peace and forgiveness, are regarded by radical Islam as signs of weakness. To many Muslims, mercy and forgiveness seem like nonsense, because to them, *revenge* is a sacred duty—this despite the fact that Muslims throughout the world portray Islam as a peaceful religion and always refer to Allah as "the Merciful."

The "Marks" in Islam

Islam carries most of the marks of the spirit of the Antichrist. First, it started in association with the Old and New Testaments. It claimed to be the outworking of that revelation of God, so it "went out" from those principles, denying certain fundamentals of the Christian faith, such as the atoning death of Jesus on the cross. Mohammed taught that Jesus did not die but rather that an angel came and spirited Him away from the cross before He died. Because there is no death, there is no atonement—and because there is no atonement, there is no forgiveness. No Muslim can have the assurance of sins forgiven.

Second, Muslims deny with fanatical intensity that Jesus is the Son of God. You can talk to them about Jesus as a prophet, and they will give you careful attention. In fact, the Quran (Koran) acknowledges Jesus as a prophet, even as a Savior, even as a Messiah. But when you say He is the Son of God, you will encounter the most intense, bitter opposition.

As I pointed out earlier, the famous mosque that is called the Dome on the Rock, built on the site of what was once the Temple of Solomon, carries Arabic inscriptions all the way around it including, twice: "God has no need of a son." Clearly, Islam denies the Father-Son relationship within the Godhead. And thirdly, Islam does not confess what the Bible says about Jesus.

In discussing the teachings of Islam, I have come to the opinion that Islam is the most sinister, powerful force in the world today opposing the truth of God. I find it a tragedy that so many Christians in the West have misunderstood and underestimated the power of Islam.

Although Islam represents such a formidable opposition, it should be said that the ultimate dominant opposition to the Lamb comes from humanism and the spirit of the Antichrist. Islam may be the most sinister and powerful force in the world *today* that opposes the truth of God, but ten years from now the picture could be different. I believe that humanism is the supreme tactic of Satan to raise up the Antichrist.

Apostate Christianity

Among the long-standing examples of the antichrist spirit, we must not omit what I call "apostate Christianity." This belief system has set aside the true biblical Jesus and replaced Him with various false representations. I call this the spirit of the Antichrist, because it pushes the true Christ out of the way and replaces Him with another. (We will examine the topic of apostasy in more detail in the next chapter.)

Both of the religions we have looked at so far—Judaism and Islam—originated in the Middle East. If you go on a tour in Israel, your guide will probably tell you at some point that the Middle East is where the three great monotheistic religions—Judaism, Islam and Christianity—originated.

This puts Christianity in the same overall category as Judaism and Islam and therefore at a high level of vulnerability to the antichrist spirit. It may well transpire that the spirit of the Antichrist will succeed in eliminating Jesus from much of the professing Christian Church, in which case we will ultimately have a Christianity without Jesus—a moral system and a legal structure that is full of all sorts of religious pageantry, but minus Jesus.

Significantly, the elimination of Jesus opens the way for a synthesis of Judaism, Christianity and Islam. I am inclined to believe that the Antichrist will head up such a religion, one that unites Judaism, Islam and apostate Christianity. Personally, I think we could be very close to this kind of unification. Over the years, both the Pope and the archbishop of Canterbury have conducted ceremonies in Christian churches where Hindu, Islamic and assorted other religious leaders were all welcomed as brothers together. The underlying purpose of these efforts is to eliminate Jesus. He is the stumbling block. The cross is the great impediment. When we read such stories in the news, we should be able to see the spirit of the Antichrist behind the façade.

Once Christians do away with Jesus on the cross, the way is open for a merger of Christianity with all sorts of religions. I believe that we are well along the way toward this kind of outcome. In my personal opinion, we need to be very discerning in our attitude and our approach to these matters, because a spirit of deception is steadily at work.

Other Belief Systems

Marxism is a political philosophy that is based on the denial of Jesus Christ. The first Marxist state, Soviet Russia, was based on a deliberate denial of Jesus Christ and all religion. Yet, in actual fact, it has really formed its own anti-Christian religious system. For everything significant in Christianity, Marxism has its corresponding evil aspect. It has its Bible (*The Communist Manifesto*), its own confessions, its "priests." Marxism is also deeply enmeshed with occult practices.

Because I live part of every year in Israel, *Transcendental Meditation*, or TM, has come to my attention as another clear expression of the spirit of the Antichrist. This belief system seems to have been more widely followed in Israel than in almost any other nation; some estimate that one out of every hundred persons in Israel has been involved in TM.

The religious sect of *Mormonism* is another example of a group that started with the Bible but has rejected the truth. The Mormons have actually built a major extension of Brigham Young University right on Mount Scopus in Israel. There was tremendous opposition to this project from the Orthodox Jews. But in the end, the Mormons succeeded.

Another simple example of the antichrist spirit at work: Many years ago, I was doing educational work in Kenya when Jomo Kenyatta was president. I have a great respect for Jomo, the first president of Kenya. But in the period leading up to the independence of Kenya, under what they called the Mau Mau Uprising, the followers of the Kenya Land and Freedom Army (known as the Mau Mau) took all the Christian hymns that the missionaries had taught them and reworded them, putting Jomo's name in place of the name of Jesus.

I am not saying Jomo was an antichrist. I believe he was a good man in many ways and did a good job, although I'm not aware that he ever became a Christian. However, it seems clear to me that the spirit at work in exalting him was the spirit of the Antichrist.

You can find much more detailed information about any of these groups and belief systems if you wish, so that you can discern for yourself the underlying influence of the spirit of the Antichrist.

4

THE RISE OF
ANTICHRIST PREDICTED

Various passages in the New Testament teach very specifically about antichrist, and I am going to deal briefly with two of them. The first is 2 Thessalonians 2, which we will use as the basis for this and the following chapter. The other, Revelation 13, will be considered in later chapters.

Preceding "The Day of the Lord"

We will examine the first part of the second chapter of 2 Thessalonians verse by verse, but you may want to read the whole chapter so you can understand the flow of Paul's teaching to the Thessalonians on this topic. I will be summarizing his thoughts as we go. Paul begins:

> Now, brethren, concerning the coming of our Lord Jesus Christ and our gathering together to Him, we ask you, not

to be soon shaken in mind or troubled, either by spirit or by word or by letter, as if from us, as though the day of Christ had come.

Let no one deceive you by any means; for that Day will not come unless the falling away comes first, and the man of sin is revealed, the son of perdition. . . .

2 Thessalonians 2:1–3

Since verse 3 speaks of the revealing of the man of sin (the Antichrist) as coming before the Lord's return, verses 1 and 2 teach us that, in effect, the manifestation of the Antichrist must precede the actual return of the Lord Jesus. Paul begins with an exhortation not to let anybody convince us in any way that the Day of the Lord (the day of the return of Jesus) has already come, because the Antichrist has not yet appeared on the scene.

In the New Testament Greek, a special word tells us that Jesus will be coming again. It is the Greek word *parousia*, which is regularly used for the Second Coming of Jesus. Interestingly, in this passage, the same word is also used of the Antichrist. So, there will be not one *parousia* but two. First of all, the *parousia* of the false [anti] christ, and then the *parousia* of the true Christ. But the *parousia* of Jesus will not take place until the *parousia* of the Antichrist has taken place.

Verse 3 begins with the words, "Let no one deceive you. . . ." How important those words are! In my view, the greatest single danger that threatens us as Christians is deception. Then the rest of that verse continues as follows:

Let no one deceive you by any means; for that Day will not come unless the falling away comes first, and the man of sin [or lawlessness] is revealed, the son of perdition.

The man of lawlessness, the son of perdition, is the Antichrist. There is only one other person who has been called by that designation in the Bible: Judas Iscariot. Judas was an apostle who turned away. This is another clear indication that the Antichrist will have some kind of association with the Church—that he will go out from the Church.

Paul makes it very clear that before the *parousia* of the Antichrist, there must be another occurrence, described by the Greek word *apostasia*, which translates into English as "apostasy." This is a specifically religious word that means a deliberate turning away from a revealed religious truth.

The "son of perdition" in this verse is also called "the man of sin" (or lawlessness). He is, as we noted earlier in 1 John 4:3, "the spirit of the Antichrist, which you have heard was coming, and is now already in the world." We notice the connection when we read Paul's words in verse 7: "For the mystery of lawlessness is already at work."

Both of these verses indicate that the spirit of lawlessness is already among us and working in our midst. However, the final, ultimate manifestation of man's rebellion against God will be the Antichrist. That rebellion will express itself when humans choose a ruler who is in rebellion against God and who is against God's appointed ruler, the Lord Jesus.

Following the "Falling Away"

Paul declares that the coming of the Antichrist will not occur until after "the falling away" takes place, which is the wording of 2 Thessalonians 2:3 used in the New King James Version. The New International Version translates it as "the rebellion." But as we noted above, the Greek word is *apostasia*, from which we get the English word "apostasy."

Significantly, *apostasy* means turning away from revealed religious truth, and Paul is teaching that the Antichrist cannot be revealed until "the" apostasy in the Church has taken place.

The reason for this is self-evident—the Church is the only spiritual barrier to the activity of Satan. This means that Satan *must* undermine the Church before he can fulfill his evil purposes.

I would suggest to you that we are living in the days of "the" apostasy. The centuries have seen countless outbreaks of wickedness, immorality, covetousness and violence in the world and in the Church. But only in this generation can we see that nearly all the major denominations of the Church have officially rejected the great basic truths of the Gospel, namely that:

- Jesus is the Son of God,
- He was born of a virgin,
- He led a sinless life,
- He died an atoning death,
- He was buried,
- He rose physically the third day,
- He ascended into heaven
- and He is coming back again.

You may or may not be fully aware of how these basic truths have been openly flaunted and denied in almost every major denomination. We see this denial not only within large denominations, but also in many smaller Christian groups.

Some years ago, some friends of my first wife, Lydia, and I attended a church of a major denomination in the United States. (I will not mention which one specifically, because this state of affairs applies to many denominations.) These friends said to us, "In our church, you can talk as much as you like about Plato or Socrates or Buddha or Martin Luther King Jr. But if you start to talk about Jesus, people get upset."

This is the spirit of the Antichrist in its first phase: "Get Jesus out of the way." The second phase is to replace Him with another. Without question, that spirit is at work in almost every area of the Body of Christ today. You and I must be able to identify that spirit so that we will not be deceived. This spirit can be very subtle; it can be very intellectual; it can be very theological. Such is the spirit of the Antichrist.

Opposing God

The Antichrist "opposes and exalts himself above all that is called God or that is worshiped, so that he sits as God in the temple of God, showing himself that he is God" (2 Thessalonians 2:4).

These verses raise a question for us to address: What is the temple of God? I have come to believe the temple mentioned here will be a physical structure built by the Jewish people on the Temple Mount in Jerusalem. I know for a fact that many Jews are actively preparing for such a building—so much so that there are actual schools for Levites to teach them how to practice the sacrifices. Making such ritualistic sacrifices is not easy. It requires knowing how to skin a sheep as well as knowing what to do with the various parts of the animal. In preparation, some people are actually weaving robes for the priests, and some have attempted to break through onto the Temple Mount (although some scholars have suggested that the actual place of the Holy of Holies was not where the Mosque of Omar now stands. Therefore, they say a temple could be rebuilt without demolishing the Mosque of Omar).

Nobody knows exactly how the verses above might be fulfilled, but it seems to be a fact that over the past few decades an intense pressure is building among the Jewish people to rebuild the Temple in Jerusalem.

A commonly known teaching in Judaism (not taught everywhere and not scriptural) declares, "The one who will give us back our temple is our messiah." By "our temple" these people mean the Temple of Herod, not the Temple of Solomon. I find it mystifying that they never go back in their thinking to the temple of Solomon but instead to the temple of Herod, because Herod was an Edomite, a wicked man who murdered many people, including members of his own family. He built this second temple only in order to accommodate the Jewish people.

My belief is that the Antichrist will at some time sit in a temple that has been rebuilt by the Jewish people. Whether or not the builders are true believers (which matters to some Bible scholars) does not sway my conviction because the Jews are God's people whether or not they are believers. And God is the God of the Jews whether or not they acknowledge Him. Therefore, if Jews build a temple to their God, then it is the temple of God.

The Restraining Power of the Holy Spirit

Paul reveals more important details:

> Do you not remember that when I was still with you I told you these things? And now you know what is restraining, that he [the Antichrist] may be revealed in his own time. For the mystery of lawlessness is already at work; only He who now restrains will do so until He is taken out of the way.
>
> 2 Thessalonians 2:5–7

As this is a matter that is discussed in numerous church circles, it demands a question from us: "Who and what is it that restrains?" I agree with those who say that this verse refers to the Holy Spirit. He is the One who "restrains." Until the Holy Spirit withdraws Himself in some way, the Antichrist cannot be fully manifested.

When that time comes, Jesus will then overthrow the Antichrist. We read in verse 8: "And then the lawless one will be revealed, whom the Lord will consume with the breath of His mouth and destroy with the brightness of His coming."

I am grateful that the true Christ will be the One taking care of the false christ, and that the task does not depend on one of us. The Antichrist is an individual of extraordinary cunning, wisdom and power, and it is completely appropriate that only the true Messiah should deal with the false messiah.

As we continue reading in the second chapter of the second letter to the Thessalonians, we come across a startling revelation in the ninth verse: "The coming of the lawless one is according to the working of Satan, with all power, signs, and lying wonders." In other words, the coming of the Antichrist will be attested to by many supernatural miracles and signs.

For years I have stated that an obvious place for the spirit of the Antichrist to arise would be in the charismatic movement. Why? Because charismatics tend to go overboard on the supernatural. Please make no mistake. I myself believe in supernatural signs and wonders. However, I do not believe that every supernatural miracle is from God. We have got to learn to discern and distinguish between good and evil because otherwise, inevitably, we will be deceived.

Moving into our next chapter, we will begin to discuss our first line of defense against such deception.

5

OUR PROTECTION AGAINST DECEPTION

When we consider the fervent opposition to the true faith that will manifest in the earth through the spirit of the Antichrist, we might be easily discouraged. However, we can count on the Lord to show us His way of salvation, especially in the midst of such difficult times.

Continuing our close reading of 2 Thessalonians 2, we see the following in verse 10: ". . . and with all unrighteous deception among those who perish, because they did not receive the love of the truth, that they might be saved."

This shows us that the best protection against deception is very straightforward: receiving and maintaining a love of the truth. Sincerely loving the truth will protect us from deception. The word for this kind of love in Greek, *agape*, is a very strong word. Used in this context, it indicates a passionate devotion to the truth.

Will it be enough for us to simply and casually read our Bibles once in a while or go to a church that preaches the

Bible? I do not believe so. You and I must esteem God's truth above all else in our lives. Many people who think of themselves as Bible-believing Christians do not exhibit this kind of love of the truth.

What Is the Truth?

The New Testament reveals three ways of understanding the truth.

First of all, Jesus says: "I am . . . the truth" (John 14:6). So, the truth is Jesus. Then in John 17:17, where Jesus is praying to the Father, He says, "Your Word is [the] truth." So, God's Word, the Bible, is the truth. Further, John says, "the Holy Spirit . . . bears witness" to Jesus "because the Spirit is truth" (1 John 5:6).

From these passages, we can understand the truth in its three interrelated aspects: The truth is Jesus; the truth is the Bible; and the truth is the Spirit. In order to know for sure that you really have the truth, you have to check all three coordinates: Jesus, the Bible, and the Spirit.

I exhort you to love God and His Word passionately. Please take more time with the study of the Bible than you take with your electronic devices or any other activity.

In equal measure, love the Holy Spirit passionately. The Holy Spirit is not an impersonal influence or a theological abstraction or a system. He is not a set of rules, nor is He a footnote in the ecclesiastical hierarchy. He is not a half sentence near the end of the Apostles' Creed. He is a Person, and He loves you.

I have sometimes summed up my view of Church history in this way: Nineteen centuries of trying to find a system so safe we would not have to rely on the Holy Spirit. But you know there is no such system. No system, no theology, no theory, no hierarchy, no human ministry can take the place of the Holy Spirit. He is indispensable. Therefore, we must cultivate a personal relationship with the Holy Spirit.

If you do not cultivate a growing relationship with the Scripture, Jesus and His Holy Spirit as a kind of "triangulation of truth," you *will* be deceived.

The only safe course for you is to love the truth. This is all-important. To be sure, it will cost you something to love the truth, because the truth will not flatter you. It may be much easier to listen to teaching that inflates your ego, making you feel you are a wonderful person. But that kind of teaching will destroy you. The only safeguard in these days is to love the truth, and to keep loving it even when it hurts. The truth will always do good things in you and for you.

Many of us are somewhat like Pontius Pilate. When confronted with the truth, we get very philosophical. We try to avoid committing ourselves to the truth, because we know it will cost us something to acknowledge the truth. Yet that acknowledgment may actually end up saving our lives because the truth will steer us away from disaster. As far as we know, Pontius Pilate never had any philosophical problems about the nature of truth until the Truth was standing right in front of him. That is when he said, "What is truth?" (John 18:38).

Pilate had not received a love of the truth, and he did not recognize Him at that crucial moment. Second Thessalonians 2:11 reads, "And for this reason God will send them strong delusion." What was the reason they were subjected to strong delusion? Because "they did not receive the love of the truth" (v. 10). And will the devil send them strong delusion? No, it will be God Himself.

As difficult as it is to believe, this is how God's Kingdom works: The ultimate judgment of God turns people over to error and delusion. We see it throughout the Scriptures.

Consider what He did with King Saul when he rejected the word of the Lord (see 1 Samuel 16:14). Concerning disobedient Israel, God poured out upon them a "spirit of deep sleep" (Isaiah 29:10). For what reason? Because the people had heard the words of the prophets but had not obeyed them.

In the verses we have been considering from 2 Thessalonians, the results of the strong delusion are extensive; they apply to the whole human race. When God sends delusions, it is impossible to believe the truth:

> And for this cause God shall send them strong delusion, that they should believe a lie: That they all might be damned who believed not the truth, but had pleasure in unrighteousness.
>
> 2 Thessalonians 2:11–12 KJV

People dislike the truth because it does not get along with their unrighteousness. We are good at coming up with all sorts of fancy explanations and justifications. We talk about the new morality or situation ethics. The fact of the matter is that we do not like the truth because it opposes the unrighteousness that wants to assert itself in every one of us.

The truth demands something of us. We cannot simply play around with the truth and suit ourselves, and then sometimes when it seems convenient decide to get back to God and receive what He has to say to us. No, we need to receive the truth and embrace it—firmly and constantly.

A Chilling Parallel

As a result of my particular involvement with Israel, I see a historical parallel in this matter of the truth. In the years immediately before Hitler came to power and in his early years in power before World War II, he was becoming more and more anti-Jewish. His bias against the Jews became evident in all of his propaganda in his speeches and in his policies.

During that time, the Zionists sent many representatives to warn German and European Jewry of what was coming. Many of them would not listen. They simply could not believe such bad things could ever happen. (Many books chronicle this era of history, and one that describes the Jewish mindset at this time is Martin Gilbert's book: *The Holocaust: A History of the Jews of Europe During the Second World War*.) Eventually, after years of denial, the forces of Hitlerism closed down on Europe and no one could escape. When that happened, millions of Jews would have given all they had to get out.

In this historical record, I see a parallel with the Christian world. We are trifling with the truth when we refuse to accept the solemn warnings and exhortations of God. Like the Jews of Europe, we may tend to view the end times as something that will never really happen in our lifetime. But what if the time comes when God will no longer plead with us, when He will no longer make the truth available to us but will instead send a strong delusion. When that happens, we will be trapped.

I feel strongly that the Lord wants me to warn you that you cannot fool around with the truth. You are not necessarily going to have another twenty years to make up your mind whether or not you want to commit yourself to God. God can shut things down in one instant—just like that—at which point, the truth will no longer be available. In that moment, even if people hear the truth, they will be unable to understand it or believe it.

Did you know that it takes the grace of God to receive the truth of the Gospel? Apart from God's grace you cannot believe. And if God withdraws His grace and sends delusion, the person upon whom it descends will be deceived regardless of how clever, religious, intellectual or philosophically sophisticated they are. In fact, the more intellectual and philosophical a person is, the easier they are for Satan to deceive.

We need to make up our minds. Are we committed to the truth? Whether we like it or not? Whether it flatters us or insults us?

I am going to make this personal. Allow me to ask you gently, as you sit quietly right where you are: Do you know the truth well and yet are not obeying it? If so, you are fooling with truth and playing religious games. Get honest and be real about it. Turn and begin to obey God's truth, which He is giving to you.

You might decide to pray something like this:

Lord Jesus, I recognize afresh the importance of truth— the truth about You, the truth of the Bible and the truth of the Holy Spirit. Forgive me for failing to receive the love of the truth that saves me from deception and protects me from delusion. I ask for Your help to stand for truth and to grow in my discernment so that I will be able to distinguish good from evil. In Your Name I pray. Amen.

Choosing Humility

Being willing to receive this love of the truth is not something you can do if you are proud. We have to set aside whatever we think we know. As Paul reminds us in 1 Corinthians 8:2, "If anyone thinks he knows anything, he knows nothing yet as he ought to know." We need to divest ourselves of all pride and recognize our need for the Lord's help in every aspect of our lives.

Please bear in mind that God will not take that step for you. You cannot pray, "God, make me humble," because God says in James 4:10, "Humble *yourselves* in the sight of the Lord, and He will lift you up" (emphasis added). How can you humble yourself? By making a decision of the will to take that action.

Let's welcome every opportunity to humble ourselves. We tend to prefer pride over humility, but only humility will release the mercy of God in our lives. When someone treats you unfairly or slanders you, what should you do? Give thanks and praise to the Lord for giving you one more opportunity to humble yourself. Remember the words of James 4:6, which echo throughout the Old and New Testaments: "God resists the proud, but gives grace to the humble."

The Bible says in Matthew 23:12 and Luke 14:11, "Whoever exalts himself will be humbled, and he who humbles himself will be exalted." Clearly, it is *your* business to humble yourself and let God exalt you. Be careful not to do it the other way around, because if you exalt yourself, God will have to abase you.

You do not want to find yourself on the wrong side of the eternal relationship with God, as Lucifer did. He was and is the ultimate rebel against God. Lucifer—the devil, the Evil One, Satan—motivates any antichrist spirit, who is known as the lawless one (see 2 Thessalonians 2:8–9).

You will recall how Lucifer, who was a glorious archangel in heaven, rebelled against God: "How you are fallen from heaven, O Lucifer, son of the morning!" (Isaiah 14:12). That name, Lucifer, means the bright or shining one. This beautiful angel became Satan, which means the adversary. It is significant that Satan started out in heaven. At first, he was one of the archangels of God. All through the story of his rebellion and fall, we see this thread: The one who belonged to God became a traitor and a rebel. Note how this links with the first mark of the Antichrist; Lucifer went out from God. Here is a picture of Lucifer's rebellion, laid bare in five statements attributed to him:

> For you have said in your heart:
> [1] "I will ascend into heaven, [2] I will exalt my throne above the stars of God; [3] I will also sit on the mount of the congregation on the farthest sides of the north; [4] I will ascend above the heights of the clouds, [5] I will be like [equal to] the Most High."
>
> Isaiah 14:13–14

Did you notice that one phrase is repeated five times? "I will, I will, I will, I will, I will." That is the essence of rebellion: my will set in opposition to the will of God.

In contrast to the wrong-hearted motivation of Lucifer, we need to understand the spirit of Jesus, which is a spirit of humble submission. One clear description can be found in Paul's letter to the Philippians:

> Have this mind among yourselves, which is yours in Christ Jesus, who, though he was in the form of God, did not count equality with God a thing to be grasped, but emptied himself, by taking the form of a servant, being born in the likeness of men. And being found in human form, he humbled himself by becoming obedient to the point of death, even death on a cross. Therefore God has highly exalted him and bestowed on him the name that is above every name, so that at the name of Jesus every knee should bow, in heaven and on earth and under the earth, and every tongue confess that Jesus Christ is Lord, to the glory of God the Father.
>
> Philippians 2:5–11 ESV

Even Jesus Christ (the Messiah, the Anointed One) did not think that equality with God was something to be grasped at. In complete contrast with Lucifer, who was a created being never equal with God but who reached for equality with Him, Jesus, who was in fact equal with God, renounced His exalted position and humbled Himself.

The satanic spirit grasps for power, authority and honor—and falls every time. The Spirit of Jesus is entitled to all power, authority and honor, but He voluntarily humbles Himself. This is the Spirit we need to follow.

You and I need to be sure that the spirit that motivates us is the same Spirit that motivated Jesus, because the spiritual forces in the world today are so strong that no one will be immune from them. If you are not filled with the right Spirit, you will be filled with the wrong spirit before long. I am not making merely a useful recommendation when I say, "You must be filled with the Holy Spirit." Being filled with the Spirit is a life-and-death necessity.

When Paul wrote in Philippians 2:9, "Therefore God has highly exalted him," what is the "therefore" there for? Because He *humbled* Himself. Jesus did not get exalted because He received special treatment as a favored Son. He was exalted because He met the conditions for elevation: He humbled Himself.

This principle runs throughout the universe, without exception. Everyone who exalts himself will be abased. But everyone who humbles himself will be lifted up.

To bring the principle home, let's consider how this works within the marriage relationship. Husbands and wives, one very good way to humble yourselves is to apologize to your spouse every time you say or do something that is out of place. Do not simply brush off your mistake. Do not shrug your shoulders and keep silent and protect your pride.

Instead, take a deliberate step, saying, "I'm sorry, my dear. I shouldn't have said that. I was unkind, I was impatient, and I was irritable. Please forgive me." Do not resist the moment—embrace it! And thank the Lord for one more opportunity to humble yourself. In this way, you will be following closely in your Savior's footsteps.

The only way to be protected from deception in these perilous times is, with humility, to receive and embrace the truth (better rendered as Truth, because truth is the person of God).

6

THE WILD BEAST FROM THE SEA

The end-times battle will have two opposing sides: Christ against the Antichrist, true against false. It will be the Lamb against the Beast, the lamb nature against the beast nature.

We already know that the Lamb of God will prevail ultimately, and as believers we want to follow Him without wavering, but how do we recognize His adversary when he appears in various disguises? How can we hold fast to the Truth (the Lord Jesus Christ) and show others how to escape the wily deceptions of the spirit of the Antichrist? Who is this "beast"? What will he look like, and what will he do?

John described what he saw in his end-times revelation. This first beast rose up out of the sea:

> Then I stood on the sand of the sea. And I saw a beast rising up out of the sea, having seven heads and ten horns, and on his horns ten crowns, and on his heads a blasphemous name. Now the beast which I saw was like a leopard, his feet

were like the feet of a bear, and his mouth like the mouth of a lion. The dragon gave him his power, his throne, and great authority. And I saw one of his heads as if it had been mortally wounded, and his deadly wound was healed. And all the world marveled and followed the beast. So they worshiped the dragon who gave authority to the beast; and they worshiped the beast, saying, "Who is like the beast? Who is able to make war with him?"

And he was given a mouth speaking great things and blasphemies, and he was given authority to continue for forty-two months. Then he opened his mouth in blasphemy against God, to blaspheme His name, His tabernacle, and those who dwell in heaven. It was granted to him to make war with the saints and to overcome them. And authority was given him over every tribe, tongue, and nation. All who dwell on the earth will worship him, whose names have not been written in the Book of Life of the Lamb slain from the foundation of the world.

If anyone has an ear, let him hear. He who leads into captivity shall go into captivity; he who kills with the sword must be killed with the sword. Here is the patience and the faith of the saints.

Revelation 13:1–10

The original Greek wording translated in the first verse as "beast" means "*wild* beast." That additional adjective makes it much clearer that this creature is fierce and destructive.

(A side note: All the creatures in the Bible that have more than one head are evil, and I do not think there is any good creature that has more than one head. In contrast, the Church has only one head: Jesus Christ.)

What does it mean that this wild beast with its seven heads and ten horns came up from the sea? My personal interpretation is that the sea refers to the world of politics, but who is to say?

This wild beast displays characteristics of three wild animals: a leopard, a bear and a lion. What do the three animals signify? Where leopards are concerned, we learn one significant biblical fact from Jeremiah 13:23, namely that a leopard cannot change its spots. In other words, a leopard cannot change its predatory and destructive nature. We cannot say categorically what the bear and the lion stand for, but there are two nations that are traditionally identified with the bear and the lion—Russia (the bear) and Britain (the lion). The wild beast portrayed here could symbolize a central European confederation made up in part by Britain and by Russia. Time will show the truth of the matter.

We will learn more about this creature through a sequence of events revealed in Revelation chapter 13.

Characteristics of the Wild Beast

Verses 2 through 7 of Revelation 13 reveal a number of identifying characteristics of the wild beast:

- Power, throne and authority (verse 2)
- Apparent resurrection (verses 3 and 4)
- Worshiped by people (verse 4)
- Significant rulership (verse 5)
- Blasphemy of the true God (verse 6)
- War with the saints (verse 7)

We also learn that the beast obtains supernatural power from Satan, who is "the dragon": "The dragon [the devil] gave him [the wild beast] his power, his throne, and great authority" (Revelation 13:2).

This wild beast goes through some kind of an experience of a death and a resurrection, and it impresses the people so greatly that they want to follow him: "I saw one of his heads as if it had been mortally wounded, and his deadly wound was healed. And all the world marveled and followed the beast" (v. 3).

I have occasionally speculated what could have happened if John F. Kennedy, the president of the United States who was assassinated in 1963, had been raised from the dead. I am sure he would have had the whole world at his feet. Although that did not happen with John F. Kennedy, something like that is going to happen at some time in the future. It may not be a real experience of a full death and resurrection. But it will prove convincing to the world, so much so that they will worship both the devil and the person with adulation, granting them even more authority. Here is the prophetic picture:

> So they [the world] worshiped the dragon who gave authority to the beast; and they worshiped the beast, saying, "Who is like the beast? Who is able to make war with him?"
>
> Revelation 13:4

Let me point out a wonderful contrast. Referring back for a moment to the fourth chapter of Matthew (the account of the Temptations of Jesus), we see another difference between the true Christ and the false one. We have seen previously how Lucifer grasped for equality with God and fell, whereas Jesus humbled Himself and was exalted to the highest place. Here we read:

> The devil took Him up on an exceedingly high mountain, and showed Him all the kingdoms of the world and their

glory. And he [the devil] said to Him [Jesus], "All these things I will give You if You will fall down and worship me."

Matthew 4:8–9

Satan has been looking for many centuries for one man whom he could empower to gain control of humanity (in order to compel the world to worship him instead of God). When the devil made his original claim of equality with God, he was thrown out of heaven so that he could no longer openly assert his claim. But there remains one way he can still assert himself as God's equal. He tries to steal the one exclusive entitlement that belongs only to God and must never be offered to anybody else—worship. If the devil can put himself in a position to receive worship, he will be able to say, in effect, "See! There you are. I'm equal with God."

When Satan suggested that Jesus give him the worship he craved, how did He respond? "Jesus said to him, 'Away with you, Satan! For it is written, "You shall worship the Lord your God, and Him only you shall serve"'" (Matthew 4:10). The true Christ turned down the temptation to worship the devil. He would not make such a bargain with Satan, even for the sake of worldly power.

What will be the difference with the false christ? When Satan offers him the same deal for unlimited power over the world, he will take it.

When the people of the world will say, "Who is like the beast? Who is able to make war with him?" (Revelation 13:4), they will be worshiping the dragon (Satan), who will have given authority to the beast. The beast will be revealed as the Antichrist, and he will seem unassailable beyond anything anyone can remember. To me, this suggests that the wild Beast will have accumulated an arsenal of catastrophically destructive weaponry, perhaps nuclear, which nobody will dare to challenge. I cannot prove my opinion, but that abhorrent prospect is not beyond the realm of possibility. We need to keep before us Scriptures such as, "Be anxious for nothing . . ." (Philippians 4:6); we are not required to be terrified because we are under Jesus' government.

This Beast will prevail over the world for a period of many months, while proclaiming boasts and blasphemies: "And he was given a mouth speaking great things and blasphemies, and he was given authority to continue for forty-two months" (Revelation 13:5). Please note the exact wording: The sentence reads, "he was given" the authority to rule with an iron fist and to blaspheme God. Who will have given him that authority? God Himself.

During this time in the not-so-distant future, the people of the earth are going to face a situation in which God permits a certain evil ruler to exercise authority for 42 months, which is three and a half years. It could well be that you will be alive through that time. We need to bear in mind that this is *God's* doing. The Bible is explicit about it. We could draw back in horror, exclaiming, "God, why would You permit this wicked man to rule the nations and to persecute true believers?" but God will not provide a full answer to that question. Nevertheless, we will have been warned that it is going to happen, and we will need to know that He has permitted it.

Some Christians believe we will be "raptured" or taken up to heaven before the Tribulation. Some people believe we will be raptured in the middle of the Tribulation. Other people believe we will go out at the end. These views are sometimes defined as pre-trib(ulation), mid-trib or post-trib. Whatever happens, I think it is important to be prepared. We can get prepared without making up our minds in advance exactly how we believe it is going to work out.

God is preparing His people for these inevitable events. I believe that the reason we are being taken through so many difficult experiences is to help prepare us for the times ahead. In the process, we are learning that we can never outthink God, nor can we manipulate Him to do what we think He should.

For example, we know that the power of God can heal any ailment, yet we do not always get healed. Why does healing often fail to occur? God does not always explain. When we experience such situations in our lives, what does it teach us? We learn to acknowledge that God is sovereign. God does what He wants to do, when and how He wants to, and He asks permission of no one. Thus we learn to trust Him and to worship Him as our Lord.

In the time that is coming, however, the beast will certainly not be inclined to submit to God's Lordship. He will be on the rampage, blaspheming not only God's name, but His dwelling place and those who dwell with Him: "Then he opened his mouth in blasphemy against God, to blaspheme His name, His tabernacle, and those who dwell in heaven" (v. 6). The wild beast will engage in open blasphemy of the true God.

Worse, he will prevail against the saints of God in warfare: "It was granted to him [by God] to make war with the saints [true believers] and to overcome them" (v. 7). Again, we see that he will do so with God's explicit permission.

The apostle Paul wrote, "If in Christ we have hope in this life only, we are of all people most to be pitied" (1 Corinthians 15:19 ESV). One of the lessons we must learn is that our hope should never be fixed on anything in this world. Our hope goes beyond time into eternity. Not everything will be straightened out in our time on earth, and we need to learn how to rest content in that knowledge.

In stark contrast to the rest of the world, we are being prepared to resist the temptation to worship the Antichrist. The rest of the world, those who have not been chosen by God to be saved, will not resist. Revelation 13:8 reveals that "All who dwell on the earth will worship him [the Beast], whose names have not been written in the Book of Life of the Lamb slain from the foundation of the world."

The only ones who will refuse to worship the Beast and Satan are those whose names were written in the Book of Life from the foundation of the world. That includes you and me, if we are believers. In other words, God preserves those whom He has chosen. If you are a believer, you believe because God has chosen you, and you can be sure that He will preserve you to the end. He will not let you down. You are not a Christian because one day you simply decided to follow Jesus. You are a Christian because God chose *you*. And that makes everything secure.

Patient Endurance by the Saints

You may have to learn this truth about your eternal security the hard way (as I have) before you can replace your anxious striving with trustful faith. Too many Christians worry and wonder if they will make it through life intact. They forget that the reason they became believers in the first place is because God chose them. They forget that He has a plan for their lives and that He will see them through.

Learning this kind of patience can be very tough. It means waiting. It involves standing back and letting things happen. It requires us to wait for God to take the initiative.

You will find that most of the great servants of God had real tests of patience. Think of Moses. Forty years on the back side of the desert, looking after some sheep. Abraham had been promised a son, but he had to wait 25 years to receive the fulfillment. David, anointed by Samuel as king, spent the next ten or twelve years as a fugitive running from the existing king.

Those who have gone before us give us insight and inspiration. We learn that certain things come only to those who are patient, and that if you are impatient, you preempt God, taking the initiative out of His hands. The writer of the book of Hebrews extols the people of the past who were people of faith. Looking to them as examples, we imitate their patient faith:

> And we desire that each one of you show the same diligence to the full assurance of hope until the end, that you do not become sluggish, but imitate those who through faith and patience inherit the promises. . . . [For example, Abraham, who] after he had patiently endured, . . . obtained the promise.
>
> Hebrews 6:11–12, 15

At some time or other in God's dealings with us, He will demand that we exercise patience because it is part of the condition of being discipled by God. After all, a teacher sets the schedule, not the pupil. As God's pupil, you do not decide when He will teach you what. He decides the when and the what. And all the time He is not merely imparting information; He is shaping your character.

Insecure believers may well follow the prosperity doctrine trail, regrettably. I consider this a troubling weakness in the theology of some contemporary Christians. Prosperity theology teaches that we can get all we want right now and thereby live in peace and prosperity for the rest of our lives. To help us refute that misguided belief, my wife, Ruth, and I once worked through the book of Job.* We noted that at the end of the book following all of the disasters and losses, God appeared to Job, and as soon as he had seen the Lord, Job had no more questions. He no longer required an explanation for every calamity that had befallen him. He found it sufficient to know that God had allowed it for reasons that were beyond his understanding.

In effect, Job's friends Eliphaz, Bildad and Zophar had based their reasonable-sounding advice on a form of the prosperity gospel. But their thinking was flawed (see Job 42:7). The prosperity doctrine claims that everything will be all right if you will simply claim it. You will never be sick. You will always have plenty of money. Everything will always work out well for you. Of course, God wants good things for us, and we should pray for them. But at the end of the book of Job, we see God's commendation of Job. He said, in effect, "Job was right." Despite Job's bitter statements about God, God applauded him for his perseverance in the face of agonizing circumstances. Job never became disillusioned. He had displayed his absolute trust in his sovereign God through his patient endurance. That was the whole point for Job, and it is the whole point for us.

We need to operate in the fear of the Lord. What God wants more than anything else is our reverent respect for Him and a willingness to acknowledge that He knows how to do His job and accomplish His purposes. He knows what He is doing. He never makes a mistake. Every choice He makes is right. Do you believe that?

He wants us to be ready for the situation portrayed in the next verses from Revelation 13:

*From our study came a book titled *Why Bad Things Happen to God's People: Making Sense of Trials & Tribulations in Your Life* (published by Destiny Image).

Whoever has ears, let them hear. "If anyone is to go into captivity, into captivity they will go. If anyone is to be killed with the sword, with the sword they will be killed." This calls for patient endurance and faithfulness on the part of God's people.

Revelation 13:9–10 NIV

If I am destined for captivity, that is where I will go. If I am due to be killed, I will be. But when such things are endured by the saints with patience and faith (for which God will supply the grace), it will not matter how badly you are mistreated. Your ultimate reward is secure, and all of the suffering will fade away in the light of eternity.

May I tell you something about endurance? The only way to learn endurance is *by enduring.* So when God puts you through challenges that you do not understand and do not like, He is teaching you endurance. You need to know how to endure if you are going to survive. He is preparing you to endure much more than you are enduring right now. Even if that does not sound like good news, can you thank the Lord right now for this preparation?

7

THE SECOND BEAST

Chapter 13 of John's Revelation portrays a second beast that appears after the first one. This evil beast arises "out of the earth": "Then I saw another beast coming up out of the earth, and he had two horns like a lamb and spoke like a dragon" (Revelation 13:11).

In my view "the earth" represents "religion." I see this beast as a religious figure. It seems to hold true to say that religion is the most powerful force in humanity. To my understanding, it follows that if Satan is going to captivate the human race, he has to have somebody religious do it. If the Antichrist is going to exercise total authority, he has to use religion as a way of attaining that dominant position.

What can it mean to say that the beast from the earth had two horns like a lamb and spoke like a dragon? It means that while claiming to be a lamb, the beast from the earth was really a dragon in disguise. He may even claim to be a follower of Jesus. But he does not act like a lamb, because he absolutely cannot—he lacks the *spirit* of Jesus, the Lamb of God.

How will believers recognize this beast? How will they be able to see through his disguise? We discussed earlier what I called the "triangulation of truth"—the triple inner witnesses of the Word of God, Jesus and the Holy Spirit. In a word, this is called *discernment*.

We Need Discernment

The Christian life should be a progression from birth to maturity. But that growth does not always happen. Too many people, after becoming Christians, do not grow in their faith, nor do they progress in their knowledge and their sensitivity to the Holy Spirit. They may learn some things, but they fail to put that learning into practice. In short, they fail to mature in their faith; their spiritual growth is stunted and their maturity is limited.

They become examples of the believers described in Hebrews 5:12—"For though by this time you ought to be teachers, you need someone to teach you again the first principles of the oracles of God." No one can master the higher truth until they have mastered the basic, underlying truth.

The Hebrew people to whom this book is addressed had had all of the privileges. They were Jewish by background. They were familiar with the Law of Moses, the Ten Commandments, the Temple service and the requirements of holiness. Even so, they had stagnated. They had made no progress. Although they should have had the ability to minister God's truth to others, they found themselves back in first grade, needing someone to teach them.

Where do you stand in regard to this question? One way to find out is to ask yourself an important question: "Do I know enough to teach somebody else?" You do not know how much (or how little) you know until you try to teach somebody else. That is the best way to find out how much Christian maturity you may have achieved.

The writer of Hebrews continues his stern reproof:

> You have come to need milk and not solid food. For everyone who partakes only of milk is unskilled in the word of righteousness, for he is a babe. But solid food belongs to those who are of full age, that is, those who by reason of use have their senses exercised to discern both good and evil.
>
> Hebrews 5:12–14

Clearly, a person can have gray hair but still be a spiritual baby, even if he or she has known the Lord for decades. Spiritual maturity is not measured by chronological age.

We need to mature in our discernment, and the only way to do that is to regularly exercise our spiritual senses to distinguish between good and evil. How does a person practice this? Philippians 1:9–11 aids our understanding. (I have translated this Scripture myself, because so few of the English versions really bring out the connection we need to make.)

> And I pray this in order that your love may abound more and more in knowledge and all discernment, that you may approve [or discern] the things that are excellent, that you may be sincere and without offense till the day of Christ . . . being filled with the fruits of righteousness which are by Jesus Christ, to the glory and praise of God.

The Greek word I have translated "discernment" is *aisthesis*, which gives us the English word "aesthetic." An aesthetic person is very sensitive to the fine points of art or music, somebody who has cultivated his or her powers of perception. This individual can walk into an art gallery and immediately pick out the works that are worthy of attention. He or she has listened to music to the point of being able to recognize music of a high quality instinctively. I think you would agree that such sensitivities cannot be developed overnight. They have to be practiced.

When we read the phrase, "sincere and without offense till the day of Christ," we may be thinking of our own potential to become offended. But verse 10 refers to behaving so blamelessly that you do not offend others, in short, demonstrating spiritual sensitivity. Instead of behaving in an offensive or spiritually coarse manner, we (looking to God for direction instead of only to other people) have learned to choose righteousness. We have cultivated the fruits of righteousness.

Our goal? To be mature in Christ and thereby filled with the fruits of righteousness, because we have cultivated spiritual sensitivity and love.

Recognizing the Best

In the context of our broader discussion of the discernment that comes with spiritual maturity, we return to the passage from Hebrews: "But solid food belongs to those who are of full age, that is, those who by reason of use have their senses exercised to discern both good and evil" (Hebrews 5:14). The word for "exercised" in this verse gives us "gymnastics" and "gymnasium" in English. How can we make sure that we are growing to full maturity in Christ? By exercising our spiritual senses.

Some Christians can be fooled by almost anything. It grieves me to discover that sometimes after I have given the very best teaching I can, the people I have taught have nevertheless misunderstood it. I am not trying to mislead them like the preachers who put a tremor into their voices to extract monetary offerings from their congregation: "Let me tell you about these desperately poor people who need your help." Or "God has shown me that there are five people here who will give a thousand dollars." I want to get up and walk out when I see preachers exploiting their spiritual position for mercenary reasons. Such tactics make me sick; and it seems to me that the people who fall for them lack even basic discernment. In a way, they deserve to be fooled.

If you get fooled once, make up your mind you are never going to be fooled that way again. You must learn to exercise your senses. Expose your mind to God's Word, because it will enable you to abound more and more in knowledge and in depth of insight. Increasingly, you will be able to distinguish between right and wrong and discern what is best.

The light of God's Word exposes subtle yet significant differences between what may seem beneficial and what will truly do us good. As Paul emphasized earlier in this passage, that light also brings forth fruit. He speaks about the fruit of righteousness that comes through Jesus Christ. As our minds are illuminated by the Word of God, we grow increasingly sensitive to what is good, to the will of God.

We must determine to grow in spiritual discernment and maturity. It is more important than ever as we confront the barrage of falsehoods and temptations in this challenging season.

Increasingly, we should be taking on the characteristics of heaven, not becoming more conformed to this earth. To repeat the one objective, scriptural fact about this Beast who arises from the earth, whoever this evil person is: He will have authority over the entire human race. His supreme aim will be to be worshiped. Why? Because when he is worshiped, the one who empowered him—Satan—will be worshiped through him; and being worshiped is the uppermost purpose in Satan's mind.

Let's be clear: Who will Satan consider to be his supreme enemies in his quest for worship? The followers of the true Messiah. The battle will be *true* against *false*. My assertion is that it will be the Beast against the Lamb. It will therefore be the beast nature against the lamb nature.

Here is how the sequence of events unfolds:

> And he exercises all the authority of the first beast in his presence, and causes the earth and those who dwell in it to worship the first beast, whose deadly wound was healed. He performs great signs, so that he even makes fire come down from heaven on the earth in the sight of men. And he deceives those who dwell on the earth by those signs which he was granted to do in the sight of the beast.
>
> Revelation 13:12–14

What one word describes the chief danger there? Deception. Why does that deception occur? Because of miraculous signs. Remember that not all miracles attest the truth of the Word of God. Some miracles affirm lies.

Note as well that miraculous power was *granted* to him. Once again, the question arises: "God, do You really mean to permit these practitioners of evil to do miracles?" Apparently, the answer from God is "Yes."

A Matter of Life and Death

I do not believe Christians, particularly in the West, sufficiently appreciate the seriousness of the situation, the fact that this is going to be a matter of life and death. We do not know just how soon these issues will emerge. But it will be "soon," and it will take place very, very quickly.

In the battle that will ensue, many saints will have to lay down their lives. Note well: "And they overcame him by the blood of the Lamb and by the word of their testimony, and they did not love their lives to the death" (Revelation 12:11). It will be more important to these believers to be true to the Lord Jesus than to stay alive.

I have taught many times on this verse because it is so strategic in overcoming the enemy. But please do not forget this one fact: It will always be more important to be true to the Lord Jesus than to stay alive.

We know that Jesus went home by way of the cross. I wonder whether the Church, in the same way, will also go home by way of the cross. We are intended to be victorious, triumphant, undefeated—but conquering by laying down our lives. Does your theology make room for that?

When I was called up into the British Army in World War II in 1940, no one ever gave me a guarantee that I would not be killed. No soldier is ever called up on that basis. When Christians talk about being soldiers of Jesus Christ, I wonder if they really understand what is involved in being a soldier. (See 2 Timothy 2:3–4.)

Before being confronted with death, the saints must discern the Beast in action. What can John mean when he describes the Beast like this?—

And he deceives those who dwell on the earth by those signs which he was granted to do in the sight of the beast, telling those who dwell on the earth to make an image to the beast who was wounded by the sword and lived. He was granted power to give breath to the image of the beast, that the image of the beast should both speak and cause as many as would not worship the image of the beast to be killed.

Revelation 13:14–15

This probably indicates something in the realm of the supernatural: an image that can speak. With present electronic achievements, this can easily be done. Even in the early years of Walt Disney World, there was a display with the speaking image of Abraham Lincoln in which he stood up and made a speech. Quite likely this talking beast will appear on a much higher level than we can imagine.

In the verses we have just cited, we see a satanic trinity. This counterfeit, unholy trinity corresponds to the Trinity of the Godhead:

- The dragon, Satan, is the counterpart of God the Father.
- The wild beast, the Antichrist, is the counterpart of the Son.
- The false prophet is the counterpart of the Holy Spirit.
- The idol that they produce is the counterpart of the Church.

As is typical for the pretender to the throne of God, this unholy trinity only imitates God. I think of the Latin saying, *diabolus simia dei* ("the devil, the ape of God"). Satan has no creative power of his own, no inventiveness.

The Mark, the Name, the Number

In the time to come, a person will have the option of being identified by only three designations: the mark, the name or the number. Without those you cannot do daily business. In effect, you are excluded from all society. John reported:

> He causes all, both small and great, rich and poor, free
> and slave, to receive a mark on their right hand or on their

foreheads, and that no one may buy or sell except one who has the mark or the name of the beast, or the number of his name.

Revelation 13:16–17

It is not that this principle of being marked is to be feared in itself as evil. Scripture tells us that the righteous will be marked as well, but they will be marked with the name of the Lord. We learn this in the description of the 144,000 saints who are mentioned in the book of Revelation. First, we read about four angels who hold back the judgment of God for a brief period:

After these things [conflict, scarcity, widespread death and cosmic disturbances] I saw four angels standing at the four corners of the earth, holding the four winds of the earth, that the wind should not blow on the earth, on the sea, or on any tree. Then I saw another angel ascending from the east, having the seal of the living God. And he cried with a loud voice to the four angels to whom it was granted to harm the earth and the sea, saying, "Do not harm the earth, the sea, or the trees till we have sealed the servants of our God on their foreheads." And I heard the number of those who were sealed. One hundred and forty-four thousand of all the tribes of the children of Israel were sealed.

Revelation 7:1–4

In other words, there must be a special company of servants of God sealed on their foreheads before this Tribulation finally explodes. Everybody will be "marked" in one way or the other.

To have the Father's name on their foreheads is a tremendous recommendation: "Then I looked, and behold, a

Lamb [remember, this is Jesus] standing on Mount Zion, and with Him one hundred and forty-four thousand, having His Father's name written on their foreheads" (Revelation 14:1). Some texts will say "having His name and His Father's name." A subsequent verse tells us: "In their mouth was found no deceit, for they are without fault before the throne of God" (Revelation 14:5).

What is distinctive about these people? They have the Father's name on their foreheads. In other words, they have apprehended what it is to have God as Father.

God does not just write truth on the pages of the Bible; God puts truth in people. We have the Bible, and I thank God for the Scripture. But Jesus said, "I am the truth." Most of us would acknowledge that truth as merely an abstract concept does not satisfy us. But we can relate to the truth in the form of a Person.

Being identified by having the name of Jesus and the name of God the Father on their foreheads shows how these people think. They are secure in the Father, identified with Him. They follow the Lamb wherever He goes (see Revelation 14:4).

This wonderful truth about the name of our Father on our foreheads is confirmed again right at the end of the book of Revelation when John is describing the New Jerusalem. In this context it is not limited to the 144,000 but to all God's servants: "And there shall be no more curse, but the throne of God and of the Lamb shall be in it, and His servants shall serve Him. They shall see His face, and His name shall be on their foreheads" (Revelation 22:3–4).

It seems to me that as this age draws to a close and as we get nearer and nearer to the time of the events pictured in Revelation, you and I will need to be sure that we will be among those who have our Father's name on our foreheads.

We are going to have to be very sure we are not looking backward. Instead, like the patriarchs, we need to be looking forward to the city that has His foundations, whose builder and maker is God.

The choice before us is this: *Whose nature will you choose?* The answer to that question determines how you will be marked. Like a barcoded item in a store, your forehead mark will show what is inside.

Calculating the Number

The passage I quoted above (Revelation 13:16–17) about the mark on people's foreheads or right hands consists of not only "the mark or the name of the beast," but also "the number of his name." What does that refer to?

The number of the name of the Beast is further explained in the next verse: "Here is wisdom. Let him who has understanding calculate the number of the beast, for it is the number of a man: His number is 666" (Revelation 13:18).

No one has conclusively figured out the exact reason for the number 666, but it is probably based on the system for the Hebrew and the Greek alphabets, as well as others, in which each letter carries a numerical value, and therefore so do names, depending upon their spelling. The correlation between letters and numbers in Hebrew is called *gematria*. In Greek it is called *isopsephy*.

The basic way it works is that the first ten letters of the alphabet represent the numbers one through ten. After that the numbers go up by tens: Ten, twenty, thirty, forty, fifty, sixty, seventy, eighty, ninety, one hundred, then up by hundreds. How high the calculations go depends upon how many letters are in the alphabet. The numerical equivalents in the Hebrew alphabet go to four hundred (although in specific cases it can go up to nine hundred). The Greek goes up to nine hundred.

Hebrew Example

Decimal	Hebrew	Glyph	Decimal	Hebrew	Glyph
1	Aleph	א	30	Lamed	ל
2	Bet	ב	40	Mem	מ
3	Gimel	ג	50	Nun	נ
4	Daleth	ד	60	Samech	ס
5	Heh	ה	70	Ayin	ע
6	Vav	ו	80	Peh	פ
7	Zayin	ז	90	Tzady	צ
8	Het	ח	100	Koof	ק
9	Tet	ט	200	Reish	ר
10	Yud	י	300	Shin	ש
20	Kaf	כ	400	Tav	ת

Using my wife Ruth's name as an example, we see from the table above that each letter has a numerical value. ("Ruth" in Hebrew is just the same in English, except the final letter is just one sound. In Hebrew it is spelled *Reish—Vav—Tav*, though from right to left.) If you write Ruth's name vertically and write opposite each letter the value of the name, then all you have to do is add up the numbers and you get the number of her name.

Reish—200
Vav—6
Tav—400
Total = 606

The number of Ruth's name is six hundred and six. (When Ruth first went to Israel, she met a rabbi there who told her, "Your name, Ruth, is a very powerful name because it has a high number.")

Greek Example

Greek is the language in which the New Testament Scriptures were written. Here are the numerical equivalents of the letters of the Greek alphabet:

Letter (upper and lower case)	Value	Name	Transliteration
A α	1	Alpha	a
B β	2	Beta	b
Γ γ	3	Gamma	g
Δ δ	4	Delta	d
E ε	5	Epsilon	e
(F ϝ / Ϛ ϛ)	6	Digamma (later Stigma)	w
Z ζ	7	Zeta	z
H η	8	Eta	ē
Θ θ	9	Theta	th
I ι	10	Iota	i
K κ	20	Kappa	k
Λ λ	30	Lambda	l
M μ	40	Mu	m
N ν	50	Nu	n
Ξ ξ	60	Xi	x
O o	70	Omicron	o
Π π	80	Pi	p
(Ϙ ϙ)	90	Koppa	q

Letter (upper and lower case)	Value	Name	Transliteration
P ρ	100	Rho	r
Σ σ	200	Sigma	s
T τ	300	Tau	t
Y υ	400	Upsilon	y
Φ φ	500	Phi	ph
X χ	600	Chi	ch
Ψ ψ	700	Psi	ps
Ω ω	800	Omega	ō
(ϡ ϡ)	900	Sampi	ts

Using this system, the name of Jesus (in Greek *Iesous*) comes out like this:

I = 10
E = 8
S = 200
O = 70
U = 400
S = 200
Total = 888

Thus, the number of the true Christ, 888, is a very significant number. The number of the false christ is 666, as we read in Revelation 13:18.

By whatever name or number, the Antichrist (the Beast in John's Revelation), is going to be a force to be reckoned with. For my part, I want to have learned how to discern him wherever he may appear, and I want to grow ever closer to the true Christ, as a bride grows ever closer to her bridegroom.

8

A PURE BRIDE

I trust that through the chapters you have read so far you have been persuaded that the Beast (the Antichrist) and the cataclysmic events of the future are all very real and very relevant to you today. These developments are not remote or from another age—they are beginning to happen here and now.

Why should they concern us? Because you and I need to know how to respond to what Satan is planning so we can stand firm. Also, since we have learned from Scripture that God is going to permit the Antichrist to have his way for a period of at least three and a half years, we need to make sure that our theology makes room for all of that. Otherwise, we will be overtaken by a situation for which we are ill-equipped.

By no means am I suggesting that the Antichrist or Satan will triumph. But I do believe there will be a period—and I believe it is the same period that is called in Matthew 24:21 the "great tribulation"—that lies ahead of us during which Satan will seem to have the upper hand. Whether your beliefs can be defined as pre-, mid- or post-Tribulation, the essence is that you should be prepared!

I am concerned that most of the Christians I know are not ready. If something serious started happening tomorrow, they would be caught unprepared. Spiritually, psychologically and emotionally, they would be unfortified against the inevitable hardships and the fear of affliction. Peter said, in effect, to the Christians to whom he wrote, "Arm yourself with the same mind; as Jesus suffered, you are going to suffer" (see 1 Peter 4:1). Only that mindset will arm you well enough to survive in the days ahead.

A Church with Muscles

As a whole, the Church is far from ready for its divine destiny. Yet I believe that Jesus wants a Church with "muscles," a Church that is not flabby or overweight. The story of Rebekah, Isaac's bride, provides a picture of such a Church (see Genesis 24).

The story is a parable of God finding a bride for Jesus Christ, His only Son. In this interpretation, Abraham, the father of Isaac, represents God the Father. Isaac, the only son, corresponds to Jesus, the only Son. Rebekah, the chosen bride, represents the Church. Another major character in the story is the unnamed servant, whom I identify with the Holy Spirit. (It always blesses me to see the Holy Spirit at work behind the scenes, never identifying Himself by name.)

When we read this story from Genesis, we see that when Rebekah came along, she drew enough water for the unnamed servant and for all ten of his camels. A camel can drink as much as forty gallons of water, which means that she could have drawn from the well as much as four hundred gallons of water. That is a lot of hard work. Rebekah must have been muscular enough to do that; she was strong and prepared. In the same way, we as the bride of Christ must be prepared to do whatever we may have to do to remain faithful to our Bridegroom.

To best prepare, we who are part of the Church must exercise our "muscles"—the qualities of godliness and maturity that we have begun to highlight in this book.

Do you remember what I referred to as our "first line of defense"—receiving the love of the truth? Satan will work "with all unrighteous deception among those who perish, because they did not receive the love of the truth, that they might be saved" (2 Thessalonians 2:10).

Receiving the love of the truth guarantees your protection from deception and destruction. God offers to us the love of the truth. Will you and I receive it? Will you and I commit ourselves to be faithful to Jesus, who is the Truth? Will we adhere to the Word of God, which is the Truth? Will we stay in step with the Spirit of Truth?

What is more, will we embrace the righteousness that comes as part of our salvation? Far from being disqualified from receiving God's gifts, every member of the Church has been declared "not guilty." By Jesus' death and resurrection, we have been justified ("just-as-if-I'd" never sinned), and that means we have been made righteous by means of God's own righteousness (see 2 Corinthians 5:21). We have been completely acquitted and cleansed. God's righteousness has no guilty past, no shadows, no consciousness of sin, no memory of sin. That is what it means to be justified by faith in Jesus and made righteous with God's righteousness.

Satan's strongest weapon against many of us is guilt. But the Gospel message is good news ("gospel" means "good news") precisely because it counteracts the guilt. Remember what Paul wrote to the (notoriously sinful) church in Corinth:

> Do you not know that the unrighteous will not inherit the kingdom of God? [That is important.] Do not be deceived. Neither fornicators, nor idolaters, nor adulterers, nor homosexuals, nor sodomites, nor thieves, nor covetous, nor drunkards, nor revilers, nor extortioners will inherit the kingdom of God. And such were some of you. But you were washed, but you were sanctified, but you were justified in the name of the Lord Jesus, and by the Spirit of our God.
>
> 1 Corinthians 6:9–11

Can you receive those words for yourself? You have been washed. You have been made clean. You have been justified. You have been made holy. You have been made righteous with God's own righteousness. Whether you were an adulterer, a fornicator or a homosexual, you have been made clean. Never let Satan make you feel guilty about those things if you have truly repented and trusted in Jesus.

People might say about you, "Well, he divorced his previous wife before he was saved, and now he's married again. So, he is living in adultery." No, you have been justified, so you are no longer guilty of the sin. I am not trying to make things easy, because I do believe in a strict morality for Christians. But I do not believe in being stricter than God is Himself.

Do you remember the vision Peter had on a housetop in Acts 10? In the vision, he saw a lot of unclean animals coming down in a sheet and was told by God to eat them. He did not want to, protesting that they were unclean. But God said, "Do not call unclean what God has cleansed" (see verse 15). We church members need to hear that. We should never dare to call unclean what God has cleansed. We should never belittle the power of the blood of Jesus, which cleanses from all sin.

As a matter of fact, our cleansing through justification and sanctification is so complete that God sees the Church as a pure virgin. Again, writing to the Corinthians, Paul employed strong words: "For I am jealous for you with godly jealousy. For I have betrothed you to one husband, that I may present you as a chaste virgin to Christ" (2 Corinthians 11:2). In the culture of those days, betrothal was not marriage, but it was as binding as marriage; it was the step just before marriage. A woman who was unfaithful in the time of betrothal was treated like an adulteress.

Paul's words are a wonderful testimony to what the blood of Jesus can do. Here Paul was speaking about the Corinthian church having become a "chaste virgin," when before their conversion they had been a group of drunkards, extortioners, liars, thieves, pimps and prostitutes. But the blood of Jesus could make them as pure as a chaste virgin bride.

Let's take these words to heart for ourselves, stepping by faith into the righteousness that Jesus has purchased for us with His own blood. This is our ultimate weapon against the incapacitating guilt Satan threatens us with.

The True Gospel under Attack

The onslaught of the enemy against the Church is relentless, yet if we respond in the right way, we become the beautiful Bride of Christ. We can then present ourselves to our Bridegroom as a chaste virgin who is strong and who loves the truth. It is only by putting on the robe of righteousness that we—because of our Bridegroom—can prevail over the "beastly" intentions of the enemy.

The prophet Isaiah put it like this:

> I will greatly rejoice in the LORD, my soul shall be joyful in my God; for He has clothed me with the garments of salvation, He has covered me with the robe of righteousness, as a bridegroom decks himself with ornaments, and as a bride adorns herself with her jewels.
>
> Isaiah 61:10

The Gospel is a pure, simple message, even though I may not always be able to communicate it that way. I would warn you against undertaking too much complicated theology. (Actually, I see theological seminaries as the main breeding ground for unbelief in the Church today. While not true of all seminaries, it is true of many. Through their influence, many Christians can end up being corrupted from the purity and simplicity of their faith in Jesus Christ.) Paul wrote, "I fear, lest somehow, as the serpent deceived Eve by his craftiness, so your minds may be corrupted from the [purity and] simplicity that is in Christ" (2 Corinthians 11:3).

I share Paul's concern as he expressed it in the next verse:

> For if he who comes preaches another Jesus whom we have not preached, or if you receive a different spirit which you have not received, or a different gospel which you have not accepted—you may well put up with it!
>
> 2 Corinthians 11:4

We must ask ourselves, "Is this the real Jesus?" because if we believe in another Jesus, then we are susceptible to the message of a different gospel and we may slip into a different spirit.

Many versions of Jesus have been peddled in the Church. One portrays Jesus as a Marxist revolutionary ("liberation theology"). This movement swept over much of South America in the middle of the twentieth century.

Another gospel pictures Jesus as a talented guru or a Buddha figure. How could the Creator of the universe be a mere guru or worshipful figurehead? Such a viewpoint opens adherents up to an entirely different gospel.

Then there is the all-too-common depiction of Jesus as a sort of Father Christmas who walks around patting people on the head, saying, "There, there! Don't worry. It will be all right."

When John described his vision of Jesus in Revelation 19:12–15, he exclaimed that He has eyes like a flame of fire and that a sharp, two-edged sword is coming out of His mouth. It should give us pause to realize that although John had known Jesus intimately in the days of His flesh, when he met the resurrected Jesus in the opening chapter of Revelation, he fell at His feet as one dead (see Revelation 1:12–17).

Make no mistake—the true Jesus is far beyond human definitions. In order to stand strong in these challenging days, we must make up our minds to receive the love of the truth and to renounce anything that conflicts with the true image of Jesus Christ. We must look for godly fellowship with like-minded believers who also love the truth. Otherwise, we are playing games and putting ourselves at risk.

Let's pray together as we conclude Part 1 of this book, committing ourselves to Jesus in a serious way, and asking Him to change us into His image.

Lord Jesus Christ, You are the Way, the Truth and the Life. The Church is Your Body and Your Bride, and You are the head over all things. Today, I want to acknowledge You. I bow my heart in Your presence, and I give You the preeminence that is due to You.

Lord, if I do not have the love of the truth, if I have been only playing around with all religious games and theories, my faith needs to be strengthened significantly. I ask You, Lord, to change me and to help me grow in spirit to become increasingly like You.

If there is anything that offends You in my life, I confess it now as sin. I receive Your justification and Your righteousness.

Have mercy on me, Lord. Have mercy on the Church in my nation. Please send a real revival that will change the Church. In Your name I ask it, Lord Jesus. Amen.

PART 2

—

UNDERSTANDING
the NATURE
of the LAMB

In Part 1, we learned about the rise of the Antichrist (the Beast) and the ramifications of that event in the world and to us as believers. I sought to provide an overall biblical picture of what kind of a person he will be, how he will operate and what he will do.

In that context, this second part describes the Lamb, who is the exact opposite of the Antichrist. As we continue to go through the book of Revelation, we can see that the contrast between these two entities generates a war between the Lamb of God and the Beast.

In the Greek of the New Testament, the word for "the lamb" is *arnion*, while the word for "the wild beast" is *therion*.

The two words are very similar in form. This emphasizes a clear balance between these two titles that is not apparent in English.

Similarly, there is a kind of balance between the revelation of the Lamb and the revelation of the Beast in the book of Revelation. It is interesting to note that in that book "the lamb" is mentioned 28 times and "the beast" is mentioned 35 times—thus providing another evidence for the balance.

In other words, these two are prototypical super-opponents. As we continue in our study, I think we will find that every descriptive term for the nature of the Beast finds its diametric opposite in the nature of the Lamb. As we move forward into describing the Lamb, we will be considering the opposite qualities to the following list. By nature, the wild Beast is . . .

cunning
deceitful
arrogant
boastful
vicious
cruel
treacherous
murderous
despotic
dominating

We will see the contrasting nature of the Lamb in the following chapters.

9

THE LAMB OF GOD

John the Baptist was sent before Jesus as His forerunner to prepare the way before Him. When the time came for John to introduce Jesus publicly to Israel, how did he describe Him? He called Jesus the Lamb of God:

> The next day John [the Baptist] saw Jesus coming toward him, and said, "Behold! The Lamb of God who takes away the sin of the world! This is He of whom I said, 'After me comes a Man who is preferred before me, for He was before me.' I did not know Him; but that He should be revealed to Israel, therefore I came baptizing with water."
>
> John 1:29–31

What does this very particular title, "the Lamb of God," tell us about Jesus?

Remember that the Israelites were very familiar with sheep and lambs, which had always been important to them traditionally, especially from the time of their exodus from Egypt onward. There was not a single Israelite listening to John for whom that word "lamb" did not have a very distinct meaning.

Every one of them would think of a lamb as a picture of meekness. Lambs are not animals that will defend themselves. They do not have talons or claws or fangs. In addition, by both their behavior and their appearance, they represent purity—clean and white. Most importantly to any Jew, in the history of Israel perfect lambs were the appointed sacrificial animals for redemption and protection. In particular, lambs were associated with one of their most solemn and important religious commemorations (still celebrated across the world today)—the Passover.

The Passover Lamb

Without a lamb there can be no Passover as it was originally ordained by God through Moses. Here is the original account of how God intended Israel to celebrate the Passover:

> Then Moses summoned all the elders of Israel and said to them, "Go at once and select the animals for your families and slaughter the Passover lamb. Take a bunch of hyssop, dip it into the blood in the basin and put some of the blood on the top and on both sides of the doorframe. None of you shall go out of the door of your house until morning. When the LORD goes through the land to strike down the Egyptians, he will see the blood on the top and sides of the doorframe and will pass over that doorway, and he will not permit the destroyer to enter your houses and strike you down."
>
> Exodus 12:21–23 NIV

The deliverance of Israel from God's judgment depended entirely upon the blood of lambs, applied around the doors of their houses. God's judgment passed over them because of the lambs' blood.

God's wrath, which would have descended upon the Israelites as well as the Egyptians, was instead deflected. It passed by because of the blood of the Passover lamb. As fulfilled by Jesus, this is a perfect picture of the significance of the Lamb of God.

Silent before Shearers

When Jesus, the Lamb of God, appeared before the Sanhedrin, He did not defend Himself in any way:

> Now the chief priests and all the council sought testimony against Jesus to put Him to death, but found none. For many bore false witness against Him, but their testimonies did not agree. . . . And the high priest stood up in the midst and asked Jesus, saying, "Do You answer nothing? What is it these men testify against You?" But He kept silent and answered nothing.
>
> Mark 14:55–56, 60–61

Jesus remained silent in the same way before Pilate, the Roman governor:

> And the chief priests accused Him of many things, but He answered nothing. Then Pilate asked Him again, saying, "Do You answer nothing? See how many things they testify against You!" But Jesus still answered nothing, so that Pilate marveled.
>
> Mark 15:3–5

This is the Lamb of God, silent before His shearers, as the prophet Isaiah had predicted:

He was oppressed and He was afflicted, yet He opened not His mouth; He was led as a lamb to the slaughter, and as a sheep before its shearers is silent [there is the picture of meekness], so He opened not His mouth.

Isaiah 53:7

Did you know that sheep really do fall silent when they are being sheared? Many years ago, I worked on a farm where there were flocks of sheep. While a sheep is being taken to be shorn, it will bleat loudly all the way. But when the shearers start clipping off the wool, at that moment the sheep becomes absolutely silent. How precise the Scripture is!

The Redemptive Blood

The blood of the Passover lamb redeemed Israel out of Egypt. The blood of Jesus, the Lamb of God, provides eternal redemption for all who believe:

But Christ came as High Priest of the good things to come, with the greater and more perfect tabernacle not made with hands, that is, not of this creation. Not with the blood of goats and calves, but with His own blood He entered the Most Holy Place once for all, having obtained eternal redemption.

Hebrews 9:11–12

Peter shows us again how the blood of Jesus obtained eternal redemption for every believer:

. . . knowing that you were not redeemed with corruptible things, like silver or gold, from your aimless conduct received by tradition from your fathers, but with the precious blood of Christ, as of a lamb without blemish and without spot.

1 Peter 1:18–19

The blood of the Passover lamb was a type—a figure. It provided temporary redemption, which had to be renewed every year. It took the blood of Jesus, the Lamb of God, God's sinless eternal Son, to provide eternal redemption. When Jesus shed His blood, it was a once-and-for-all sacrifice that never had to be repeated. Jesus had obtained eternal redemption for all of humanity.

The Nature of the Lamb

Because Jesus was the perfect Lamb of God, you and I, along with all of His redeemed ones, need to "put on the Lord Jesus Christ" (Romans 13:14).

The pure, meek nature of Jesus as the Lamb of God sets an example and a pattern that we must learn to follow in our lives, with the help of His Holy Spirit. Here is Peter's exhortation about this:

> For to this you were called, because Christ also suffered for us, leaving us an example, that you should follow His steps:
> "Who committed no sin,
> Nor was deceit found in His mouth";
> who, when He was reviled, did not revile in return; when He suffered, He did not threaten, but committed Himself to Him who judges righteously.
>
> 1 Peter 2:21–23

This is the Son of God, standing before His accusers, offering no defense, no retaliation, displaying His lamb nature. As believers, we are called to follow in His steps. We too must reproduce that lamb nature. When He bestowed His Spirit on us, He implanted His very nature into us.

This lamb-like nature can also be associated with another creature—the dove. When John the Baptist baptized Jesus in the Jordan River, the Godhead told him that the One upon whom he would see the dove descending and remaining— that would be the long-awaited Messiah. John watched as a dove descended upon his cousin, Jesus, whom he immediately declared to be the Lamb of God (see John 1:29–32). John's declaration speaks of the connection between the nature of the lamb and the nature of the dove.

Note that it was not just that the dove would settle on Jesus' head. The dove would remain on Him. Jesus never did anything to scare the Dove away. The same needs to be true for you and me. If we want to have the anointing of the Holy Spirit upon us, we must continually carry the nature of the Lamb. The Holy Spirit (the Dove) will never come to us because of our human nature. But if He sees the nature of the Lamb in us, then He is willing to settle on us. And if we want the Holy Spirit to remain upon us, we should continue to operate out of the nature of the Lamb.

Having been associated with the Pentecostal movement for many decades, I have seen the Holy Spirit come upon many people and many ministries. But on very few of them did He remain. Why? Because, essentially, they "frightened" the Dove away by failing to maintain the nature of the Lamb.

In their natural makeups, both lambs and doves will never fight. They are entirely meek and peaceable. I believe as Christians we need to learn from this. I often hear people praying for "power," and I thank God for the supernatural power of the Holy Spirit. But power is not what we need the most. *Our most crucial need is the nature of the Lamb.* Do we value it highly enough? Sadly, I do not think so. In fact, that truth has been almost forgotten in many parts of the Church.

Please let me remind you again that every one of us is going to have to make a decision: We must determine which nature will control us. The spirit of the Antichrist is actively at work, seeking to take over all of humanity. It is true to say that if we do not cultivate the nature of the Lamb, we *will* come under the power of the Beast. These are our only two options: the Lamb or the Beast.

10

War between the Lamb and the Beast

I have learned something about the devil: One of the things he hates the most is to be exposed. So what I seek to do throughout this book is to expose him in the light of Scripture. Already he does not like me, and I guarantee you that he will object. However, I do not intend to stop now. (And I have been doing just fine without his favor!)

I hope that you understand clearly that you and I are in the midst of a conflict between two spiritual forces: the Spirit of the Lamb and the spirit of the Beast. Today we must make the decision concerning which one will govern us. It will be too late to change our minds later, when the Antichrist makes himself known.

In other words, by our attitudes and the way we live and relate to others today, we determine our destiny. At some point, all the world is going to be confronted with a simple choice between the Lamb and the wild Beast. But by then, the choices will have been made, because we need to have made our decision *before* that time comes. In that day, everybody not under the banner of the Lamb *will* be under the Beast's, by default. Even now, we can discern those who are under the Lamb, because more and more they manifest the Spirit of the Lamb. But those under the Beast will become his victims when he appears on the earth; and they will not have a second chance to choose.

This is why your choice today and the way you live now is so critical.

Called, Chosen, Faithful

John describes the war that the forces of the Beast have declared on the Lamb and those who are with Him:

> The ten horns which you saw are ten kings, who have received no kingdom as yet, but they receive authority for one hour as kings with the beast. These are of one mind, and they will give their power and authority to the beast. These will make war with the Lamb, and the Lamb will overcome them, for He is Lord of lords and King of kings; and those who are with Him are called, chosen, and faithful.
>
> Revelation 17:12–14

This war is one of the main themes of the book of Revelation.

Please notice the kind of people who are with the Lamb (Jesus Christ). Those who are with Him are *called*, *chosen* and *faithful*. Let's focus on those three characteristics for a moment.

You will remember that Jesus said, "Many are called, but few are chosen" (see Matthew 20:16 and Matthew 22:14). In other words, a lot of people are invited into the Kingdom of God, and they may accept the invitation. But if they do not fulfill the requirements of their calling, they will not be chosen. This is true of a missionary calling. Multitudes of people have been called over the centuries, but many of them were never chosen. Why? Because they did not meet the conditions or fulfill the requirements of their calling.

But after being chosen there is one more requirement—to be faithful. I have been a Christian probably longer than most people. I know that we talk a lot about the problems of young Christians. But I want to tell you, they are nothing compared with the problems of *old* Christians. I do not imagine that the Christian life will ever get easier. It seems to get more complicated and demanding the further you go. The pressures increase. Some people find it impossible to remain faithful in the face of all the complications, even though God stands ready to grant increasing strength and grace to meet the pressures.

Do you want to serve in the army of the Lamb? Well then, once you are called and chosen, you will have to rely on His grace and empowering to remain faithful to the end.

The Issue of Control

Every fallen human being possesses a desire to take control, to rule and to dominate. Actually, that impulse was put in us by the Creator, because He commanded our first parents, Adam and Eve, to rule the earth. But that original directive from God became corrupted early on, with their fall into sinful disobedience. Now all around us, people want to dominate and control others.

This is the motive for all the wars in history. Ambitious people want to control other people, and the others fight back to preserve their autonomy. This impulse rises up in every one of us, without exception, because we are all sinful human beings. Even within the Church, we see struggles for control and all kinds of contention. Preachers try to manipulate their congregations. Factions develop. Power struggles ensue.

We can see it in the conflict Moses had with the magicians of Egypt before Israel could be delivered. Just as Jannes and Jambres (whose names have been remembered because of the significant nature of their opposition) came against Moses, so in our age practitioners of the occult will resist the messengers of the Gospel. Paul condemns them specifically in one of his letters to Timothy:

> Now as Jannes and Jambres resisted Moses, so do these also resist the truth: men of corrupt minds, disapproved concerning the faith; but they will progress no further, for their folly will be manifest to all, as theirs also was.
>
> 2 Timothy 3:8–9

By "these . . . men of corrupt minds, disapproved concerning the faith," Paul is referring to the long list of sinful "control issues" that will sound familiar to us:

> But know this, that in the last days perilous times will come: For men will be lovers of themselves, lovers of money, boasters, proud, blasphemers, disobedient to parents, unthankful, unholy, unloving, unforgiving, slanderers, without self-control, brutal, despisers of good, traitors, headstrong, haughty, lovers of pleasure rather than lovers of God, having a form of godliness but denying its power. And from such people turn away! For of this sort are those who creep into households and make captives of gullible women loaded down with sins, led away by various lusts, always learning and never able to come to the knowledge of the truth.
>
> 2 Timothy 3:1–7

Whether these behaviors originate from sinful human hearts or in overt occult practices, they are controlled behind the scenes by Satan. This familiar, natural tendency toward improper control follows after the nature of the wild Beast. I find it alarming that so few people understand the implications.

This is a picture of the close of the age. The real battle between the forces of Satan and the forces of Christ will be fought in the supernatural realm. But praise God, the Bible declares that the folly of Satan's administrators will be openly manifested and that the Church will be on the winning side in the showdown between Kingdom and occult powers.

"Not by Might, Not by Power, but by My Spirit"

This matter of the choice between the nature of the wild Beast or the nature of the Lamb is a spiritual one. You and I can make decisions with our minds, but in the final analysis, this is a spiritual decision. We decide to cede control of our lives to the Lord Jesus Christ or to His adversary, the devil; we give ourselves to one spirit or the other. No one can make the decision for us.

There will not be any "takeovers." In the world of business, we hear about takeovers, usually "hostile takeovers," when one corporation tries to take over another. This is never how the Spirit of the Lamb operates, even when the "taking over" is happening in the context of the Church.

At times in my ministry, the Lord has sent me to developing nations or nations that have been under communism or other oppressive regimes. I have considered it imperative to warn the people in those nations against any ministry that comes in with the intention of taking over. (Many such ministries come from the United States, but also from Canada,

Britain, Sweden and other developed nations.) My message was unequivocal: "Do not submit to them. They are not sent by God." Any ministry that wants to take over comes from a spirit other than the Spirit of the Lamb, even if they use the Name in their presentations.

In other words, the Lord makes things happen not by physical strength, military might, political power or domination. God's Spirit works in a different way. Through the prophet Zechariah, God said, "Not by might nor by power, but by My Spirit" (Zechariah 4:6).

The Way Up Is Down

Jesus explained to His disciples how God's Spirit works:

> You know that the rulers of the Gentiles lord it over them and those who are great exercise authority over them. Yet it shall not be so among you; but whoever desires to become great among you, let him be your servant. And whoever desires to be first among you, let him be your slave—just as the Son of Man did not come to be served, but to serve, and to give His life a ransom for many.
>
> Matthew 20:25–28

Here is a simple principle of the Kingdom of God: The higher up we want to go, the lower down we have to start. If you desire to be great, you have to be a servant. But if you want to be *first*, you have to be a *slave*. What could be more opposite to the way the world works? What could be more contrary to our own carnal nature? Such is the nature of the Spirit of the Lamb.

This mindset is too often missing in the Christian circles in which I move. Instead, everybody talks about power, leadership principles, extending ministry, taking over churches, forming larger organizations. I do not believe this way of thinking comes from God.

In practical terms, how can you and I begin to enter into the nature of the Lamb? How can we surrender to the Lamb's way of doing things, serving the Body of Christ like a servant? We must start by surrendering everything that we currently do in the name of Christ.

At one point in my ministry, I had to make a major decision concerning all of my teaching material. We are talking about hundreds of audio and video messages that had been produced over many years, along with several years' worth of radio programming, including a program in Chinese and Mongolian, and a large number of books. I felt that God was indicating that I should no longer administrate the distribution of it. I said to Him, "All over to You. I have no claims on it. I will not try to control it—You are in charge of it, and You can do what You will with it."

As a result of that surrender, I have been amazed at the way the ministry has expanded. I had no worries about it. I did not have to keep it going, because I had placed it in the hands of the Lord. In place of that former focus, God then gave Ruth and me a different sort of ministry—the ministry of intercession, which to us was a very exciting development. We could see that He was moving us into His own hidden ministry in heaven. Jesus had about thirty years of ordinary family life, three and a half years of public ministry and now over two thousand years of intercession from heaven:

> Who is he who condemns? It is Christ who died, and furthermore is also risen, who is even at the right hand of God, who also makes intercession for us.
>
> Romans 8:34

If anyone sins, we have an Advocate with the Father, Jesus Christ the righteous.

1 John 2:1

He is also able to save to the uttermost those who come to God through Him, since He always lives to make intercession for them.

Hebrews 7:25

Because our Lord is an intercessor, each one of us should be an intercessor as well, serving behind the scenes to advance the Kingdom of God. This is one way that we demonstrate the true nature of the Lamb.

11

STRENGTH IN WEAKNESS

As we humble ourselves and seek the way of the cross, we find ourselves in a place of perceived weakness. That is not a comfortable place to be, but Scripture speaks about it frequently. We can learn a lot from the apostle Paul's experiences of hardship and weakness.

The other apostles had plenty of hardships. But Paul seemed to have had problems wherever he went. When he came to a city, revival or revolution—or both—ensued. Time and time again, he was beaten, imprisoned, expelled from a city or stoned. I believe that Paul had been assigned a satanic angel who followed him around stirring up trouble.

Amazingly, however, it was through this very opposition and resulting weakness that Paul found true strength:

And lest I should be exalted above measure by the abundance of the revelations, a thorn in the flesh was given to me, a messenger of Satan to buffet me, lest I be exalted above measure. Concerning this thing I pleaded with the Lord three times that it might depart from me. And He said to me, "My grace is sufficient for you, for My strength is made perfect in weakness." Therefore most gladly I will rather boast in my infirmities, that the power of Christ may rest upon me. Therefore I take pleasure in infirmities, in reproaches, in needs, in persecutions, in distresses, for Christ's sake. For when I am weak, then I am strong.

2 Corinthians 12:7–10

It seems paradoxical at first. But it is part of the nature of the Lamb to convert weakness into strength. In fact, it is a spiritual law: *God's strength is made perfect in our weakness.* When I am weak, then I am strong. Do you see how God has to bring you to the place of weakness before He can reveal His strength for you? And when you have no strength, it becomes very obvious that the strength you have has come from God.

I have learned this by experience. Every time I preach, I say to God, "In myself, I have nothing to give. I am totally dependent upon You. If *You* do not give me something, I have nothing to offer." And I add, "God, only what comes from Your heart—through my heart to the heart of the people—is of any value whatsoever."

Consistently, I have found that God comes through. He answers this prayer. Sometimes, however, I forget to pray beforehand. I have stopped right in the middle of delivering a message to ask myself, *"Did I acknowledge my dependence upon God before I started to preach?"* I will gladly stop for a moment in order to acknowledge my dependence upon Him. Then I have new strength for the task at hand.

Let's examine other Scriptures and examples, both from the characters of the Bible and personal experience, to better understand this mystery of how God's strength is made perfect in our weakness.

Paul's Adversities

To be sure, Paul's extensive missionary journeys gave rise to many unprecedented, seemingly damaging incidents that make sense only when we see how God worked them out. For example, think about what happened when he was in Philippi (see Acts 16:16 and following). There, Paul and Silas and some other believers got up every morning and quietly went to a morning prayer meeting. But each morning on the way, a young slave girl with a spirit of divination (the Greek refers to a "python spirit") followed them, and she was not quiet, shouting after them: "These men are the servants of the Most High God, who proclaim to us the way of salvation" (Acts 16:17).

Now, while she was proclaiming the truth, she was motivated by Satan, not the Holy Spirit. And Paul could tell. The Bible tells us that he got "greatly annoyed" (v. 18). (If Paul and Silas had been like some modern missionaries, they would have made her a charter member of the church in Philippi. But Paul knew better.)

Another term for the slave girl with the spirit of divination is fortune-teller. As a fortune-teller, she could apprehend spiritual truth supernaturally, and her owners were able to make a good profit from her fortune-telling abilities. But a fortune-teller's truth-telling is like bait that conceals a hook. Paul knew this, and he knew she was stirring up trouble. (Before Ruth was my wife and before she knew the Lord, she had an experience with a fortune-teller. This woman knew nothing about her, yet she was able to tell Ruth three details about herself that were absolutely true: "You are unable to bear children. Your husband has left you. You have three children." Each of those statements was true. Every one of them was supernaturally revealed—from Satan.)

Paul did not want anybody to take the bait. So one morning, exasperated, he turned and addressed the spirit of divination directly. Notice that he did not rebuke the girl herself, only the evil spirit: "I command you in the name of Jesus Christ to come out of her!" (v. 18). And it did. Immediately, she lost the power to tell fortunes.

This was good, right? Not as far as the slave girl's owners were concerned. They had just lost a lucrative sideline. That is when all the trouble started. This young girl had made a lot of money for her masters by telling fortunes. So her owners seized Paul and Silas and dragged them before the authorities in the marketplace:

> And they brought them to the magistrates, and said, "These men, being Jews, exceedingly trouble our city; and they teach customs which are not lawful for us, being Romans, to receive or observe." Then the multitude rose up together against them; and the magistrates tore off their clothes and commanded them to be beaten with rods. And when they had laid many stripes on them, they threw them into prison, commanding the jailer to keep them securely. Having received such a charge, he put them into the inner prison and fastened their feet in the stocks.
>
> Acts 16:20–24

I see that rage-filled reaction as more than natural—to me, it is supernatural evidence that Satan was behind the scenes the whole time, trying to impede Paul's ministry.

In the rest of the sixteenth chapter of Acts, we find out how God converted the seemingly weak position of Paul and Silas into surprising strength. This is the story of how, after they had been beaten and thrown into the prison, they rejoiced—and at midnight an earthquake shook all of the prisoners free. The prison-keeper knew this was God's doing, and he was converted on the spot, along with his family. And the next day, having been fed and having had their injuries cared for by the jailer's family, Paul and Silas were free to say their good-byes to the Philippian church and depart for the next city.

Only in God's Strength

You and I may never have the same experiences as Paul and Silas or the other first-century disciples. But we have the same God, who is building the same Kingdom in the midst of the same messed-up world the early disciples encountered. In the twenty-first-century scene, only the characters have changed; the spiritual principles are the same as they were in Paul's day.

In the Spirit of the Lamb, we must be humble and teachable, whether we find ourselves in a high position or a low one. We must learn what it takes to bring the light and the love of Christ into unfamiliar and even antagonistic situations. This requires the crucifixion of our personal egos, which otherwise end up crippling our outreach.

In 1957, I was the principal of a college in Kenya that trained African teachers. Seven different tribes contributed students to our college, each one with its own language and culture. I myself was British, not African, and I was sharply aware of all of the differences between us. But God gave me a supernatural love for the people of Africa.

One of my goals was to immerse myself in the thinking of these people. I discovered the best way to do so was when I was teaching English, because I would assign them to write compositions in which they would have to let me know what they were thinking. Do you know what I discovered? Every one of those tribes secretly believed they were better than all the rest. Even though they were all Africans, they were, in essence, guilty of racism and a form of nationalism.

They made negative assumptions about each other, and each tribe favored itself over the others. It is similar to what we do when we say, "All Americans are loud," or "All British people are too reserved and formal" or "All Germans are bossy." We do not stop to think about which spirit—the Spirit of God or the spirit of His enemy—our preconceived suppositions come from. We rarely recognize that our egos need to be crucified and our opinions muted so that we can better love the people around us with God's love. We may sometimes go through the right motions and say the right words, yet we wonder why there is no real fruit in our lives and ministries. We are insensitive, and proud of it.

My first wife was Danish, and I know the Scandinavian peoples well. I am grateful to them because I owe so much to them. But in my experience, Swedes are proud of their nationality to an unhealthy degree. Of course they have many good points, but what this shows me is that carnality—the unredeemed and unsanctified human nature—has free rein in every corner of the earth.

You and I have been reborn into new life, and the Spirit of the Lamb needs to rule our lives, with the fruit of the Spirit—love, joy, peace, patience, kindness, gentleness, and self-control (see Galatians 5:22)—as the evidence.

Our personal strength is absolutely insufficient to do the work of God. We must surrender ourselves to Him, not only once at the beginning of our Christian walk, but daily as we discover how weak we really are. In the long run, the fountain of seeming strength that springs from our egos will dry up.

Whether we find that we have a problem with selfishness or irritability or bigger matters, such as deeply entrenched prejudice, let's allow the Holy Spirit to shine His light wher-ever He desires and by whatever means He chooses. If He seems to have led you into a dead end and you do not know what to do next, remember Paul and Silas. Rejoice in every situation, because you are not your own. You belong to the Lamb, and He is shaping you into His image.

12

WRITTEN ON HUMAN HEARTS

As we deal with certain aspects of the nature of the Lamb in these chapters, have you noticed how often the topic of the Holy Spirit keeps coming up? The Holy Spirit and the nature of the Lamb are one. That is why the nature of the Lamb becomes established in our lives only in direct partnership with the Holy Spirit. Paul put it this way:

> Clearly you are an epistle of Christ, ministered by us, written not with ink but by the Spirit of the living God, not on tablets of stone but on tablets of flesh, that is, of the heart.
>
> 2 Corinthians 3:3

Paul is identifying the fruits of his ministry by exemplifying the Corinthian believers who had started out more wicked than others but who now led lives of purity and holiness. Something profound had occurred in their hearts, and it showed in the way they lived their lives.

This "epistle of Christ" to which Paul refers is written by the Holy Spirit on the hearts of men and women. Who else can write on a human heart except the Holy Spirit Himself? I can pour out many words as I preach or write, but only the truths the Holy Spirit writes on the hearts of my listeners and readers will prove beneficial. The transformation that takes place through the power of the Holy Spirit goes much deeper than the emotions or the intellect. It goes right to the core of one's being.

Another way of saying it is that as we mature in Christ Jesus, we develop the nature of the Lamb. We abandon our personal ambitions and stop taking advantage of people. Our new way of living involves looking out for the needs of others before our own. Paul's exhortation finds a home in our transformed hearts:

> Let nothing be done through selfish ambition or conceit, but in lowliness of mind let each esteem others better than himself. Let each of you look out not only for his own interests, but also for the interests of others.
>
> Philippians 2:3–4

This mature unselfishness can be hard to find in the Church. Many expressions of Christianity are full of personal ambition, as revealed by the liberal use of personal pronouns. "This is *my* ministry." "These are *my* gifts." "This is *my* church." "This is *my* message." "These are *my* converts."

I think we could admit that the nature of the Lamb has not been well-nurtured in the Church.

The Weakness and Foolishness of God

Most of us have been brought up to rely on our own strength, to compete and get ahead of others and to depend upon our own rational thinking. But Jesus shows us a completely different way.

Paul's perspective was that "the foolishness of God is wiser than men, and the weakness of God is stronger than men" (1 Corinthians 1:25). In the eyes of the world, our desire to receive the nature of the Lamb sounds foolish. And yet the essence of God's foolishness is the cross of Christ. To the world, a Lamb that was slain is a contemptible thing. They think that this Jesus was a good man, possibly even a prophet from God, but He died the death of a criminal. He did not fight back. His followers scattered. What a picture of weakness and failure!

But the world cannot see into the hearts of those followers. The cross worked in their hearts in the early Church, and it is working in our hearts today.

The way of the cross is not cheap. But it is priceless. There is no amount of money that will buy what God offers freely if you will meet His conditions. Surely the whole thing seems counterintuitive. When John was in the midst of his grand revelation, he might have expected to see God as a Lion. But instead, he saw a Lamb, a sacrificial Lamb.

Against all expectation, a *Lamb* had all of the authority and power. A Lamb occupied the highest position in the universe. The whole of creation was worshiping a slain Lamb.

What a picture of strength in weakness! It shows us what God is looking for—broken, yielded spirits, people who will trust Him and follow Him even when nothing is working out the way they expected.

Learning to Trust Him

Those whose hearts have been changed will trust the One who changed them. Their trust and obedience will prove that

Jesus' death and resurrection rectified the original *mis*trust of our first parents, Adam and Eve, who chose to believe the devil's lie that God was not treating them fairly and that they should therefore become autonomous. The enemy persuaded them that they could find much greater personal significance if they would only eat the fruit of the Tree of the Knowledge of Good and Evil.

When they turned away from God in the Garden and helped themselves to the fruit, they ceased to trust Him. Ever since, trusting Him has been difficult for human beings, especially when hardships and tragedies predominate in their experience.

The book of Job tells a story about trust. Some years ago, I preached a series of three messages called "Why Do These Things Happen to God's People?" that was based on the book of Job. The second time I delivered this series of messages, Ruth had to remain in our apartment in Florida, grappling with the agonizing pain of a back injury. She was learning to trust God right in the midst of a Job-like experience. More recently, a friend of ours was cruelly injured in an accident that should never have occurred, and he was in danger of losing his eyesight. Shortly after the incident, we spoke to him on the phone, and he said, "Derek, I want to thank you for that message, 'Why Do These Things Happen to God's People?' I have been walking it out."

I am trying to convey a simple message: When circumstances do not work out the way we would prefer—or even when things happen exactly opposite of what seems right—we need to learn Job's lesson. What pleases the Lord most in difficulties is when we say, "Lord, I still trust You. I don't understand. But I trust You."

The perfect example of that response is Jesus—cruelly betrayed, insulted, abused, in agonizing physical pain. He was nailed to a cross and abandoned by His friends—and ultimately by His Father. Yet, He still trusted Him.

If you really want to please your Father in heaven, *trust Him.* That is what He is looking for. It is the only way back from the Fall, when humankind fell away from trusting God. Restoration means we start trusting Him again, in every circumstance.

Restoration means putting things back in their right place and right condition. And the very fact that restoration is needed is sufficient evidence that things have been out of their right place and condition. If we talk about restoring an ancient building, that is sufficient evidence that the building needs repair. It is not in the condition in which it ought to be. The fact that God's people need restoration is evidence in itself that they have not been and are not at this time in the condition in which God intends them to be.

To show us our need for restoration, God will often put us through very challenging circumstances. Psalm 102 captures it well: "He weakened my strength in the way; He shortened my days" (v. 23). He is not punishing us for disobedience or sin—we are walking "in the way," after all—but the suffering is very real.

At some point as I meditated on this verse, the Lord showed me that I had put the emphasis on the wrong word ("weakened"). Instead, I should have put it on "my"—"He weakened *my* strength in the way." God weakens my strength so that I will make room for *His* strength. The strength being weakened is my own, not the Lord's, and this means that the situation is improved, because God's strength is being made perfect in my weakness.

If we are honest with ourselves, we will admit that this is disturbing news. But it comes down to trust. Do we trust that the Lord is working in our lives with eternity in view?

He loves us. He is sovereign over us. Whenever you are going through some kind of struggle as the psalmist was, remember that God is still on His throne and He knows what He is doing—even when He is weakening your strength.

"Do Not Take Your Spirit from Me. . . ."

In King David's penitential psalm, penned after he had been convicted of his defiling sins of adultery and murder, he cried out, "Do not take Your Holy Spirit from me" (Psalm 51:11). He did not pray, "Restore Your Holy Spirit *to* me"; instead, he said, "Do not take Your Holy Spirit *from* me." Then he prayed, "Restore to me the joy of Your salvation" (v. 12).

He had lost his joy, but not God's Spirit. If God had taken the Holy Spirit from him, he could never have repented. It was the very fact that God permitted the Holy Spirit to remain with David that enabled him to repent.

This means that the Holy Spirit will dwell in an unclean vessel—under certain conditions. You do not have to be perfect to be filled with the Spirit. Sometimes Christians support the unscriptural doctrine that you have to be perfect to have the Holy Spirit, or that having received the Holy Spirit makes you perfect and complete. Not true. *Well*, they think self-righteously, *I have received the Holy Spirit. I must therefore now be perfect!* The problem with that assumption is that then I have to *act* as if I am perfect in every situation. So, for example, I no longer lose my temper; I just have "righteous indignation." Besides, a pretense of perfection can put other people off. ("Well, if that's the standard, then it's hopeless. I can never attain that. It's just too much for me. I'm not even going to try.") Anyway, other people see right through it, especially when they see us stumble.

Sometimes influential people can fall into that misconception. During Billy Graham's first crusade in Britain at London's Harringay Arena in 1954, I heard this statement from a well-known evangelical Bible teacher who is now with the Lord: "About receiving the Holy Spirit and speaking in tongues—you would have to be very holy to receive that." This is simply not true!

You do not have to be perfect. Nobody is perfect; in fact, most of us are far from perfect. But we do need the Holy Spirit, and once we have received Him, God will never take Him away. Nor did He take Him from David, nor from anyone else whom He has called to Himself.

Think, for example, about the Gentiles who gathered in the house of Cornelius (see Acts 10). Nobody in the house had ever heard the Word of God before. They were Gentiles. But they *all* received the Holy Spirit that day. Why? Because they were thirsty. That is one primary condition for receiving the Holy Spirit. Jesus said, "If anyone *thirsts* [not if anybody is perfect], let him come to Me and drink" (John 7:37, emphasis added).

Yielded Will, Broken Spirit

King David explained what God is looking for, and His conditions are quite different from what we might expect. David expressed the truth when he wrote, "The sacrifices of God are a broken spirit, a broken and a contrite heart—These, O God, You will not despise" (Psalm 51:17).

I find that statement amazing. I recall vividly my first encounter with this truth. I was saved in an army billet in 1941 and was soon afterward sent out to the Middle East. In 1942, I took my first leave from the British army, and I went to Jerusalem. There I met an American Assemblies of God pastor who happened to be an Assyrian by background. His name was Saul Benjamin. Saul took pity on this poor soldier who did not know where to go or what to do; he and his family welcomed me into their home. (Saul Benjamin is the one who baptized me in the Jordan River on August 24, 1942. Two photographs show first the pastor and me, both in black robes, standing in the river, and second the pastor in the river with a splash where I had just gone under.)

Something Saul said to me in a casual way has never faded from my memory: "There's a difference between a yielded will and a broken spirit." When he said that, something registered with me, and I said, "That's got to be true. I do not understand it, but I believe it."

About a year later, I found myself in the Sudan. During my time there, I led a Muslim called Ali to the Lord. He was in charge of the local labor force in the hospital where I was working. Ali was the second person I had ever led to the Lord, and his conversion was so dramatic that all the British people in the hospital exclaimed, "What's happened to your friend Ali?"

I said, "He got saved."

When they responded with, "What's that?" I got to tell *them* about salvation, too.

After Ali came to faith, a very unpleasant turn of events took place. To explain, let me say that when you are in the Middle East, you will find sooner or later that it is often a place of lies. People do not speak the truth naturally. My first wife, Lydia, who spent twenty years among the Arabs, used to say: "When an Arab speaks to you"—and she did not say this out of prejudice against anybody, but just as an objective fact—"he doesn't think, 'Is this true?' He thinks, 'If I say this, how will the other person respond?'" Words become a means to provoke the response you want from the other person, not a way to express the actual truth.

In the matter of my friend Ali's conversion, a lie was disseminated in the hospital about him. It was reported that he had done something very wicked. When I heard it, my heart really broke for Ali. A lot of things happened in that situation that could have caused me to become very angry, but I simply held my peace. Later I discovered that what had been said was a lie. It simply was not true. But I had seen a glimpse of what it is to have a broken spirit. A broken spirit does not argue, does not fight back, does not justify itself, does not make claims. That is the heart attitude God looks for.

My beloved reader, if you yield to the Lord, you can expect that He will bring you, sooner or later, to circumstances that will break your spirit. When you get there, do not protest and make demands. Do not object, saying, "This is a colossal mistake. Something must have gone wrong." Realize that God's end purpose is to deal with your character. He is forming the nature of the Lamb in you, and a broken spirit is an essential element of the Lamb's nature.

13

THE KEY TO PURITY
AND HOLINESS

L et's take a deeper look at the passage in Revelation 5
that describes when John first saw the Lamb:

And I saw in the right hand of Him who sat on the throne a
scroll written inside and on the back, sealed with seven seals.
Then I saw a strong angel proclaiming with a loud voice,
"Who is worthy to open the scroll and to loose its seals?"
And no one in heaven or on the earth or under the earth was
able to open the scroll, or to look at it.

So I wept much, because no one was found worthy to open
and read the scroll, or to look at it. But one of the elders
said to me, "Do not weep. Behold, the Lion of the tribe of
Judah, the Root of David, has prevailed to open the scroll
and to loose its seven seals."

And I looked, and behold, in the midst of the throne and
of the four living creatures, and in the midst of the elders,
stood a Lamb as though it had been slain, having seven horns
and seven eyes, which are the seven Spirits of God sent out

into all the earth. Then He came and took the scroll out of the right hand of Him who sat on the throne.

Now when He had taken the scroll, the four living creatures and the twenty-four elders fell down before the Lamb, each having a harp, and golden bowls full of incense, which are the prayers of the saints. And they sang a new song, saying:

"You are worthy to take the scroll,

And to open its seals;

For You were slain, and have redeemed us to God by Your blood

Out of every tribe and tongue and people and nation,

And have made us kings and priests to our God;

And we shall reign on the earth."

Then I looked, and I heard the voice of many angels around the throne, the living creatures, and the elders; and the number of them was ten thousand times ten thousand, and thousands of thousands, saying with a loud voice: "Worthy is the Lamb who was slain to receive power and riches and wisdom, and strength and honor and glory and blessing!"

Revelation 5:1–12

At first, the apostle John was weeping because no one was able to open the scroll. But then one of the elders told him there was indeed a Person who could open the scroll of revelation. He said, "Do not weep. Behold, the Lion of the tribe of Judah, the Root of David, has prevailed to open the scroll and to loose its seven seals."

John looked at the throne, expecting to see a lion, but what did he see? A lamb. A slain lamb.

What is the message? Only the Lamb has the right to be on the throne, because He has all authority in heaven and on earth. And how did He obtain supreme authority? As the multitude sang: "You are worthy to take the scroll, and to

119

open its seals; for You were slain, and have redeemed us to God by Your blood. . . ." (v. 9).

Because He offered Himself as a perfect sacrifice, the Lamb is utterly worthy—not only to open the sacred scroll, but also to "receive power and riches and wisdom and strength and honor and glory and blessing" (v. 12).

Later, in Revelation chapters 7 and 14, we read about a very special company of 144,000 believers. Concerning them, Revelation 14:4–5 says: "These are the ones who follow the Lamb wherever He goes. . . . They are without fault before the throne of God."

What is the key to purity and holiness? To follow the Lamb wherever He goes. But you cannot follow the Lamb if you have the nature of the Beast. Only if you cultivate the *nature of the Lamb* can you follow Him.

Years ago, I had a friend who had grown up in what is called the apostolic movement in Wales. He had been a minister in that movement, but he became disillusioned because he was exposed to a great deal of boasting and very little reality in their movement's claims. He was also troubled when he saw people competing with one another for the top positions. Then he read about the New Jerusalem in Revelation 21:14, which helped him understand why he was troubled: "Now the wall of the city had twelve foundations, and on them were the names of the twelve apostles of the Lamb."

Quoting the verse, he stated, "I've made a discovery about apostles. They're not on top of everybody, holding them down. They are in the foundation, at the bottom, holding others up."

Still today, there are a lot of people calling themselves apostles. For many, that designation provides a good excuse for holding others down. But a true apostle is at the bottom. His strength does not lie in holding others down. Rather, his strength, which is really the Lord's strength in him, is in lifting others up.

In their own following of the Lamb of God, apostles are meant to be our examples, are they not? Paul wrote, "Follow my example, as I follow the example of Christ" (1 Corinthians 11:1 NIV). Whether or not you and I have been called to be apostles, we, too, should be representing the Lamb more and more perfectly as we mature spiritually. The question is: How do we do that? In practical terms, how can you be sure you are growing into the nature of the Lamb?

Knowing God through His Word

This statement may be self-evident: You and I do not naturally think the way God thinks. The prophet Isaiah reminded us of this fact:

> "For My thoughts are not your thoughts, nor are your ways My ways," says the LORD. "For as the heavens are higher than the earth, so are My ways higher than your ways, and My thoughts than your thoughts."
>
> Isaiah 55:8–9

Truly God's ways are higher than our ways and His thoughts higher than our thoughts. And one of the primary means by which He shows us His ways and His thoughts is through His Word.

He does not want us to be deceived into thinking that our salvation is a static condition, arrived at by going forward at the altar of a church, saying a little prayer and shaking the pastor's hand. It is a caricature of salvation to think that all it involves is exchanging the label "sinner" for a tag that reads, "saved." Salvation is not a static condition; it is a dynamic way of life, as more than one Scripture states clearly, for example:

> The path of the righteous is like the morning sun, shining ever brighter till the full light of day.
>
> Proverbs 4:18 NIV

> Nevertheless, the righteous will hold to their ways, and those with clean hands will grow stronger.
>
> Job 17:9 NIV

The Lord wants each of us to grow into all that He has in store for us. In fact, you could say that the Christian life is supposed to be a *living* thing, continually growing and bearing fruit. It is not static. It does not just hold on to what it has or bury itself in the ground protectively (see the parable of the talents in Matthew 25:14–30). Our life is meant to be a life of *multiplication*: "Grace and peace be multiplied to you in the knowledge of God and of Jesus our Lord . . ." (2 Peter 1:2). This multiplication comes only through the knowledge of God and of the Lamb of God, Jesus. Everything we ever need is channeled to us through God and through Jesus. We do not need any other ultimate source of supply: "as His divine power has given to us all things that pertain to life and godliness" (2 Peter 1:3).

Stop right there and take note of the tense of the verb. In the Greek language, it is the perfect tense, which shows us that God has already given to us all we are ever going to need for time and eternity—for every area of our lives. Everything we will ever need that pertains to life and godliness has already been given to us by the Lord.

As it turns out, you and I pray on the basis of a misunderstanding much of the time. We ask God to give us something

He has already given us. It is not easy for God to answer those prayers, because in answering them, He would support the underlying misunderstanding. Sometimes we have to adjust our thinking in order to pray the kind of prayer God desires to answer.

The second half of 2 Peter 1:3 conveys a point that is of critical importance: ". . . through the knowledge of Him who called us by glory and virtue." Please notice that the glory included in the knowledge of Jesus Christ is not *our* glory, but rather *His*. Not *our* virtue, but rather *His*. In the Greek this comes through clearly: ". . . called us *to His own* glory and virtue."

So God has already given us everything we will ever need and it comes to us through the knowledge of Jesus. The Greek word translated above as "knowledge" can equally be translated "acknowledging"; the word means both knowledge and acknowledging.

This shows us that it is not merely that we intellectually know about Jesus. It means that we also effectively acknowledge Him in every area of our lives.

Verse 4 contains the next vital part of this revelation: ". . . by which have been given to us exceedingly great and precious promises." *God has already given* us everything we are going to need. Where is that provision? In His promises, in the promises of His Word. Simply put: God's provision is in His promises. If you and I can grasp that principle and apply it, the effect on our Christian walk will be life-changing.

Then at the end of verse 4, we encounter another breathtaking statement: ". . . that through these [the promises] you may be partakers of the divine nature." I do not know how it could be said any better. Peter is saying that you and I can receive the actual nature of God. We, too, can become divine. You might say, "It seems outlandish to say that." Yes, it does.

But in one of the psalms, we read, "I [God] said, 'You are gods, and all of you are children of the Most High'" (Psalm 82:6). Jesus, when He was challenged about being the Son of God, quoted that psalm when He said, "He called them gods, *to whom the word of God came* (and the Scripture cannot be broken) . . ." (John 10:35, emphasis added).

Do you see it? Because the Word of God comes to us through the promises of God, we can become partakers of God's nature. We can become divine. I realize that statement can be misused. But I believe that in the way I have presented it, this truth is an accurate representation of what Scripture teaches.

Returning to 2 Peter, let's put it all together:

Grace and peace be multiplied to you in the knowledge of God and of Jesus our Lord, as His divine power has given to us all things that pertain to life and godliness, through the knowledge of Him who called us by glory and virtue, by which have been given to us exceedingly great and precious promises, that through these you may be partakers of the divine nature, having escaped the corruption that is in the world through lust.

2 Peter 1:2–4

The last few words, ". . . having escaped the corruption that is in the world through lust," show us that in the same proportion to which we become partakers of the divine nature we will be delivered from the corruption that is in this world. The divine nature and corruption are incompatible. The divine nature is incorruptible, while everything in this world is corruptible. As His children, born from above, we become partakers of the nature of God through the promises contained in His Word, and we are delivered from the world's corruption that we were first born naturally into.

This is a genuine revelation, and its scope is such that you cannot absorb it just by skimming the words. Here is a summary:

- God's divine power has already given us everything we are ever going to need for time and eternity.
- It comes through knowing/acknowledging Jesus.
- The provision of God is found in His promises.
- As we appropriate the promises, we become partakers of God's divine nature.
- And as we become partakers of God's nature, we are delivered from the corruption of this world.

God's divine nature is the nature of the Lamb. The corruption of this world is the nature of the Beast. We choose to grow *in the nature of the Lamb* by following Jesus intimately and by immersing ourselves in the truth of the Word of God, under the guidance of the Holy Spirit.

The Charter of the Kingdom

As I was considering how I could best depict the nature of the Lamb from Scripture, I felt directed by God to the Sermon on the Mount, which is recorded in the fifth chapter of the gospel of Matthew. In the Sermon on the Mount, Jesus spoke about eight types of people He called "blessed," and we call these statements the Beatitudes.

As a Christian leader, I have met scores of believers who are seeking God's blessing. However, relatively few of them realize that they have to meet certain conditions. The astounding fact is that if you meet the conditions, you do not even have to seek the blessing, because the blessing will come to you as a matter of natural course! As Moses said to Israel, "If you fulfill these commandments, the blessing of God will come upon you and overtake you" (see Deuteronomy 28:2).

Although the principles in the Beatitudes overturn popular opinion about blessedness, they can be considered the charter of the Kingdom of God. In effect, Jesus preached that the citizens of the Kingdom of God will be enabled to behave in the way He describes.

Someone in our household once placed the words, "Be attitude" on one of our mirrors. That is a fairly accurate summation of the Beatitudes, because they describe what we should *be*.

At the same time, we should never forget that we cannot "be" virtuous simply in our own strength; we need the help of the Holy Spirit.

Blessed are the poor in spirit.

"Blessed are the poor in spirit, for theirs is the kingdom of heaven" (Matthew 5:3).

Very few people think it is a blessing to be poor, so they find Jesus' statement to be startling, even though Jesus was not speaking about financial poverty as much as He was about *spiritual* poverty.

In the New Testament, God is said to be rich in two qualities: *mercy* and *grace*. The poor in spirit are those who realize how desperately they need the mercy and the grace of God. They know they are not rich without them.

The Greek word that was translated "poor" means "beggars." We must ask ourselves direct questions: Am I a beggar, spiritually? Or am I rather satisfied with myself? Do I consider that I have come a long way in life and that I am doing pretty well? Do I feel that I am doing somewhat better spiritually than most of the people around me? As you might guess, if that is how you feel, you are *not* poor in spirit.

Blessed are those who mourn.

"Blessed are those who mourn, for they shall be comforted" (Matthew 5:4).

Normally, nobody considers it a blessing to mourn. But Jesus said those are the ones who get blessed. The ones who are sorrowful, the ones who grieve, the ones who humble themselves, the ones who empathize with the grief of others—they will be comforted.

Mourning is the way we were designed to release our grief. Mourning releases our grief instead of shutting it up inside. And if we fail to mourn, we will not be comforted; it is as straightforward as that. We will miss out on the blessing.

I read a newspaper article which suggested that people spend more time on funerals and mourning than necessary. That kind of sentiment is typical of the present age, where we measure value by the amount of time we give to something. This kind of thinking has no place in the second beatitude, because mourning is essential in our lives, and the comfort that comes our way in response assuages our grief best.

Blessed are the meek.

"Blessed are the meek, for they shall inherit the earth" (Matthew 5:5).

God does not offer His Kingdom to those who are arrogant or self-assertive. He offers it only to those who recognize that in themselves they are unworthy. In her song of triumph, Hannah, the mother of Samuel, declared these words: "He [God] raises the poor from the dust and lifts the beggar from the ash heap, to set them among princes and make them inherit the throne of glory" (1 Samuel 2:8). A thousand years later, the virgin Mary, in an even greater song of triumph, proclaimed the same truth: "He has put down the mighty from their thrones, and exalted the lowly" (Luke 1:52).

Who is going to inherit the earth? The *meek*. Not the strong; not the grabber; not the self-promoter. It will be the meek, and they will win by *yielding*.

As long as we are operating in our own strength, we do not make room for God's strength. God increases strength to those who have no strength (see Isaiah 40:29. Only when we come to the end of our strength and surrender to God can His strength take hold. When you come to the end of your own strength and reach out to God, you are meek.

Meekness is a word that has almost dropped out of contemporary usage. But it is still just as valuable as ever. The meek do not appropriate the earth. They do not dominate the earth. They *inherit* the earth. This makes it a test of our faith. Are you and I willing to let God allot our inheritance without grabbing for it and without fighting for it?

Blessed are those who hunger and thirst for righteousness.

"Blessed are those who hunger and thirst for righteousness, for they shall be filled" (Matthew 5:6).

Especially to typical Middle Eastern thinking, that is an absurd and paradoxical statement. Hungry and thirsty people do not consider themselves blessed.

Note that Jesus did not say it is good to hunger and thirst after peace or joy or healing or deliverance or prosperity. In my travels, I meet many Christians who hunger and thirst after those things. However, comparatively few of them hunger and thirst for righteousness.

Once you have entered into righteousness, peace and joy will follow as a natural consequence. Our aim should not be to go for peace or joy apart from righteousness, "for the kingdom of God is not eating and drinking, but righteousness and peace and joy in the Holy Spirit" (see Romans 14:17). If we make righteousness our aim, these other blessings will follow.

Blessed are the merciful.

"Blessed are the merciful, for they shall obtain mercy" (Matthew 5:7).

Throughout my walk with the Lord, I have always realized that I need the Lord's mercy. There has never been a day in my life as a believer when I have not been aware of my need for the mercy of the Lord. By nature, I am not a very merciful person, but I have decided to be merciful to others—because I want God to show mercy to me. I need it desperately.

In the light of a verse from Titus, it is interesting to consider the previous beatitude, which speaks of righteousness, along with this beatitude, which speaks of mercy: "Not by works of righteousness which we have done, but according to His mercy He saved us, through the washing of regeneration and renewing of the Holy Spirit" (Titus 3:5). God's blessing has not come to us by works of righteousness which we have done, but solely due to His mercy. Every person desperately needs the mercy of God, and I will gladly put myself at the top of that list.

Whenever I am tempted to be unmerciful, unkind, critical—whenever I am tempted to withhold the good that I could do to others—this beatitude always comes to me.

Blessed are the pure in heart.

"Blessed are the pure in heart, for they shall see God" (Matthew 5:8).

Purity of heart is the most important part of holiness, and without holiness, no one will see the Lord (see Hebrews 12:14).

The point is not to keep a set of religious rules, but rather to have a heart that is pure. Man-made rules never change a person inwardly.

The writer of the letter to the Hebrews explained how God brings us to holiness and purity of heart—through His discipline: "[Our human fathers] disciplined us for a little while as they thought best; but God disciplines us for our good, in order that we may share in His holiness" (Hebrews 12:10 NIV).

Purity and holiness do not result only from abstaining from sin and impurity. God imparts to us His very nature, and we become pure in heart as a result. That purity brings us into the very presence of the Lord.

Blessed are the peacemakers.

"Blessed are the peacemakers, for they shall be called sons of God" (Matthew 5:9).

Peacemakers can quell strife, and the most effective ones do it by means of the wisdom God imparts to them. James addresses this "wisdom that is from above" (3:17) as the antidote to human disputes:

> Where envy and self-seeking exist, confusion and every evil thing are there. But the wisdom that is from above is first pure, then peaceable, gentle, willing to yield, full of mercy and good fruits, without partiality and without hypocrisy. Now the fruit of righteousness is sown in peace by those who make peace.
>
> James 3:16–18

Peacemakers manifest the Lamb's wisdom and serenity because they share in the nature of the Lamb.

Blessed are those who are persecuted for righteousness' sake.

"Blessed are those who are persecuted for righteousness' sake, for theirs is the kingdom of heaven" (Matthew 5:10).

Do you consider being persecuted as an indication of blessing? Jesus went on to tell His disciples:

> Blessed are you when they revile and persecute you, and say all kinds of evil against you falsely for My sake. Rejoice and be exceedingly glad, for great is your reward in heaven, for so they persecuted the prophets who were before you.
>
> Matthew 5:11–12

This final beatitude defines the criterion for "blessed persecution," namely being persecuted "for righteousness' sake." Scripture tells us that everyone who lives a godly life in Christ Jesus will suffer persecution (see 2 Timothy 3:12). But it is important to draw the distinction between persecution for righteousness' sake and judgment for wickedness.

Persecution for righteousness' sake comes upon the righteous from the wicked. Judgment for wickedness comes from God, who is righteous, upon the wicked. While we are all called to endure persecution, believers should never have to endure God's judgment upon the wicked. Do you understand the distinction? Especially in the present times at the end of this age, we need to be confident that we belong to the Lamb. From His perspective:

> . . . the time is at hand. He who is unjust, let him be unjust still; he who is filthy, let him be filthy still; he who is righteous, let him be righteous still; he who is holy, let him be

131

holy still. And behold, I am coming quickly, and My reward is with Me, to give to every one according to his work.

Revelation 22:10–12

Now is the time, in view of the escalating conflict between the Lamb and the Beast, to choose the righteousness of the Lamb over the corrupted counterfeit of the Beast. We will grow in the nature of the Lamb only as we follow Jesus closely, placing our steps as He directs us, immersed in the truth of His Word as illuminated by the Holy Spirit.

14

THE LAMB WINS

As we have seen, there are many references to the Beast and the Lamb throughout the book of Revelation. In fact, these figures—the wild Beast and the Lamb—are presented a total of 63 times. They are at war with one another, not only in the end times, but also in the present outworking of our lives here on earth. To our eyes at present, the battle is intensifying, and the aggressor, Satan, seems to be winning. However, if we read to the end of the book, we find out who wins—*the Lamb*!

That outcome is contrary to all natural expectations, because at this point all the power appears to be on the other side; everything seems to be arrayed against the people who want to live for God. But we are "more than conquerors through Him who loved [and who loves] us" (Romans 8:37).

I believe this is an important message for God's people in this age. If we behave like the wild Beast—grabbing, fighting, asserting our rights, making demands—we will surely lose. If we turn to the Lamb and lay our lives down and say,

"Here I am, God. Be it unto me according to Your will and according to Your Word," we will win in the end, along with all of the forces of the Lamb of God.

How can it be that the most powerful being in heaven is a *slain Lamb*, the slain Lamb we read about in Revelation 5:1–12? To be slain means He was dead, and something dead is completely powerless.

Yet this Lamb who was slain also rose from the dead. He did not bring Himself back to life—the Father raised Him from the dead by the power of the Holy Spirit.

Are we willing to take the same pathway? To die and stay dead until God raises us back to life? When you and I are raised back to life in that way, we lead a very different life from before, the life of the Kingdom of God. This is the life of the Lamb who was slain, and it is an overcoming life.

The way of the Lamb is a way of death to life. This is the way we must follow to the throne of heaven, where the saints who have gone before us are assembled to proclaim the worthiness of the Lamb:

> Then I looked, and I heard the voice of many angels around the throne, the living creatures, and the elders; and the number of them was ten thousand times ten thousand [which is one hundred million], and thousands of thousands [which is millions], saying with a loud voice: "Worthy is the Lamb who was slain to receive power and riches and wisdom, and strength and honor and glory and blessing!"
>
> Revelation 5:11–12

The way to the throne is the way of the cross and the tomb. Only after that shall we, by the will of God, experience resurrection and ascension. It cannot happen by our own efforts.

The Way of Death

Why are so many Christians struggling to succeed and survive? Because they are striving in their own strength. Because they have never experienced death. They have not yet become willing to let go and let God. They have never experienced God's resurrection power in their life.

I am not talking about the baptism in the Holy Spirit, as wonderful as that experience is. I am talking about a level of living where we can say, "It is no longer I who live, but Christ lives in me; and the life which I now live in the flesh I live by faith in the Son of God, who loved me and gave Himself for me" (Galatians 2:20).

This death-to-life Christianity is so real we cannot help but proclaim, "Worthy is the Lamb!" Along with all the host of heaven and the saints who have gone before us, we, too, lift up our voices in praise of the Lamb who was slain.

It is imperative to have the big picture in our hearts and minds as we walk through the day-to-day realities of the life of faith. Walking as Jesus walked is not always easy, but it is always good. This nature of the Lamb is irresistible as a force for good. While we may experience what feel like setbacks, there is something far deeper at work. In a word, we who were once dead have been revived.

Looking toward Revival

"Revival" is not just a religious word; it is a personal reality. By the grace-infusing application of God's truth, our personal revivals feed Church-wide revival. God has in mind the whole world, and at the same time the most insignificant-seeming individual believer. Only by the collective effect of individuals surrendering to His Lordship will the Church and the Kingdom become fully revived.

My prayers for revival were ignited many years ago. In 1953, when I was pastoring a very small congregation in Bayswater, London, I awoke one night at about two o'clock in the morning. (That seems to be the time God wakes me when He has something He wants to say to me.) That time, He woke me by speaking to me audibly. I am not implying that God's audible voice is necessarily more authoritative than any other way in which He speaks. But it was fairly unique for me.

He did not make any introduction. He simply made certain statements—and the first statement was this: "There shall be a great revival in the United States and Great Britain."

To be truthful, in those days I was not the least bit interested in the United States. It was before the days of jet travel, and we had very little money for travel anyway. As far as we were concerned, the United States was a remote country.

Then the Lord spoke briefly to me about my own ministry. I have never felt free to share the details of what He said, but He closed with these words: "But the condition is obedience in small things and in great things, for the small things are as great as the great things."

Afterward, I went to the Bible and made a study of the topic of "small and great." What I learned was that almost everywhere in the Bible where small and great are mentioned, "small" comes *before* "great."

Because of God's word to me about revival in the United States and Great Britain, I also read and studied a certain amount about revival. I observed that the coming of revival seems to be conditional. The primary condition always necessary for God's people to fulfill is *obedience*.

136

By extension, obedience can be said to put small actions before great ones. Sometimes obedience involves taking actions that may seem very silly or unrelated to a great issue such as revival.

Sometime later, I was interviewed by a team from UCB Radio in England. One of their questions to me was, "What do you think about Britain? Is there a possibility of revival?"

I said, "Yes, I believe there is." I am very British at my roots, and I am deeply concerned for my own country, the nation of Great Britain. We began to discuss "revival" as the interview continued.

To illustrate a point, I used a wonderful example that had become very vivid to me. I had been in South Africa years before, and someone there had told me about an area of South Africa called *Namaqualand*. It is a very dry area, and very little grows on it. In fact, it can remain desperately arid and barren for years on end. But at rare intervals, heavy rains fall on Namaqualand. Right after those rains have fallen, there is the most gorgeous display of flowers you can see anywhere in the world. The reason for this phenomenon is that the seeds that have lain dormant beneath the soil, unable to germinate because of the lack of moisture, suddenly burst forth into glorious life.

I told the interviewer, "I believe Britain is like Namaqualand. It is dry and barren. But under the surface, there are seeds of biblical truth. Over Britain's long history, that nation, as far as I understand it, has had more exposure to the truth of the Bible than any other nation on earth. The seeds are still there. Once the rain falls, we will be astonished at what comes up. That is my belief. That is my vision. And I pray for its manifestation every day."

That is revival—a coming to life from apparent deadness. Many people talk about revival as if it is synonymous with evangelism, but I feel that the two need to be distinguished from each other. While I believe passionately in evangelism, it is not the same as revival.

Revival means bringing back to life something that has died. Evangelism is presenting the truth to people who have *never had life*. Revival brings back to life people who once had life and then died. Evangelism brings the life-giving Word to unconverted people.

Revival is for the Church. Once revived, the Church can reach out effectively in evangelism. (The Church is the Body of Christ, and Christ is its Head. Therefore, God redeems the lost through the Body.)

Meeting God's Conditions

People are always prophesying revival and I am not altogether sure that is helpful, because it may promote an attitude of, "Well, since revival is coming, we don't need to do much about it." Let's remember that revival does not come until we meet God's conditions. The sovereign will of God requires the members of the Body of Christ to engage with Him, which will enable them to meet His conditions.

The chief way believers in the Church meet His conditions is through cultivating the nature of the Lamb in their lives. The characteristics of the nature of the Lamb—righteousness, meekness, purity, holiness, the fear of God, truthfulness, and more—come only through God's grace. These are characteristics of both individual revival and corporate revival.

Do you see how it all works together? Since revival is a sign that we are approaching the end times but since we cannot achieve true revival without the Lord's intervention, we must reach out to Him in obedience (often in small ways, which combine to become larger ways). By doing so, we are choosing the Lamb and repudiating the Beast, even before the final coming of the Kingdom of God.

Revival opens the door to large-scale evangelism, which is another signal that the end times are upon us. "Evangelism" means "spreading the Good News," and clearly, the end purpose of evangelism is to bring sinners into the Church. But we do not want to bring new believers into an un-revived Church. First, the Church must be revitalized, revived, made alive.

When Billy Graham came to Harringay for his London Crusade in 1954, I served as a counselor in those meetings. I counseled 22 people who made a commitment to follow Jesus Christ, and I kept a record of each person who made that commitment, because we were required to follow up with them, staying in contact by phone, by letter or by other means. I did as well as I could to follow up with them, but eventually I was forced to conclude that probably only two people out of that number had become really committed Christians. (As it turned out, they both joined my congregation, even though I had not persuaded them to do so, and I believe that being brought under the teaching of the Word of God was vital to their survival.)

We can be as energetic as possible in our evangelism, but what kind of church are we going to invite the new converts into? At that time, some rather cynical Christians made this comment: "It doesn't make sense to put a live chick under a dead hen." Our first priority must be to revive the hen. Then the chick will survive. Would you agree?

In the great 1904–1905 Welsh revival, leader Evan Roberts used this slogan: "Bend the Church and bow the world." I believe that is true. If the Church will bend, the world will bow. The destiny of the nations depends on the Church. Will we bend in surrender to the Lamb? Will we meet His conditions and become revived? Will we succeed in bringing the Good News to a dying world? Will we be ready?

How Will Revival Change the Church?

I see two key ways in which revival will change the Church: (1) We will recognize Jesus as the Head, and (2) the Church will understand her role as the Bride of Jesus Christ.

Jesus Is the Head

Paul made it clear that God "gave [*gave*, not imposed] Him [Jesus] to be head over all things to the church, which is His body" (Ephesians 1:22–23).

To my understanding, the function of a head is to make the decisions and take the initiative. I would suggest that there seem to be very few areas in the Church today where Jesus is permitted to make the decisions and take the initiative. The initiative seems to have been taken out of His hands and placed in the hands of human leadership. Unfortunately, there seem to be very few serious attempts to find out what the Lord has planned.

In one of my books, *The Destiny of Israel and the Church*, I wrote a sentence that was a surprise, even to myself. Sometime after the book was published, in fact, I noticed it and asked myself: "Did I write that?" In essence, what I said is this: *God only endorses and blesses that which He Himself has initiated.*

I have observed that the programs and plans God has initiated will flourish. They grow, and they have life and power. We must understand that it is the height of presumption for us in the Church to take the initiative out of the hands of Jesus Christ.

Thankfully, some groups do place the initiative in His hands and follow His lead. But not many. We need a widespread revolution in this regard if the Church is ever going to be revived; Jesus must truly become head over all things to the Church.

Years ago, I preached on this issue of the headship of Jesus at our church. It was one of those occasions when I stepped beyond what I planned. I said to the church members, in particular to the leaders, "You have to decide who is head. Are you willing to let Jesus in so that He can really make the decisions and plans?" The next week, the header at the top of the church bulletin read, "Come on in, Lord Jesus." I believe that response was a move in the right direction.

The Church Is the Bride of Christ

When the Church is revived, we will gain a heightened understanding of the Church as the Bride of the Lamb. We find this terminology in the book of Revelation:

> And I heard, as it were, the voice of a great multitude, as the sound of many waters and as the sound of mighty thunderings, saying, "Alleluia! For the Lord God Omnipotent reigns! Let us be glad and rejoice and give Him glory, for the marriage of the Lamb has come, and His wife [or bride] has made herself ready."
>
> Revelation 19:6–7

Please notice that the bride has to have *made herself ready*. Do we today see a Church diligently making herself ready? In most places, there is very little evidence that this is happening.

How does this work? How is the Bride supposed to make herself ready? "And to her it was granted to be arrayed in fine linen, clean and bright, for the fine linen is the righteous acts of the saints" (Revelation 19:8). In other words, the material to be used for our wedding dress is *our righteous acts*. Without righteous acts there will be no fine linen. Without trying to sound flippant, it seems to me that the contemporary Church has only enough material for a bikini—far from suitable as a wedding gown. How long will it take for us to produce sufficient righteous acts to match our profession of faith?

As I understand it, when you and I believe in Jesus Christ as our personal Savior, His righteousness is imputed to us. But imputed righteousness is not the same as the *outworked* righteousness that Revelation 19:8 is talking about. Our imputed righteousness needs to be expressed (outworked) in righteous acts.

One obvious righteous act that is of particular concern to me is proclaiming the Gospel of the Kingdom in every nation. If the Church does not do that, we cannot expect to be ready for the wedding.

When Jesus is truly regarded as Head of the Church, and we start to fulfill our role as the Bride of Christ, we will begin to see that we are firmly taking on the character and nature of the Lamb.

The Lion and the Lamb

We read in Revelation 5:5 about how John fully expected to see a strong lion (the Lion of Judah) open the sealed scroll:

> But one of the elders said to me, "Do not weep [or do not go on weeping]. Behold, the Lion of the tribe of Judah, the Root of David, has prevailed to open the scroll and to loose its seven seals."

Expecting to see what the angel had described—a powerful Lion—John must have been surprised instead to see a slain Lamb:

> And I looked, and behold, in the midst of the throne and of the four living creatures, and in the midst of the elders, stood a Lamb as though it had been slain, having seven horns and seven eyes, which are the seven Spirits of God sent out into all the earth. Then He came and took the scroll out of the right hand of Him who sat on the throne.
>
> Revelation 5:6–7

This is a tremendously powerful revelation. John was expecting to see a powerful predator, a lion. When he looked, however, he saw a Lamb—not only a meek and gentle Lamb, but a Lamb that looked as though it had been slaughtered. Then the text goes on to describe how this Lamb is positioned right at the throne with the One who sits on the throne, and how He is at the very center of the worship of the whole universe.

✳ The truth portrayed here is a continuing lesson—in fact, an eternal lesson—that in order to conquer, you first must yield. In order to receive life, you first must lay it down. ✳ Strength derives from weakness.

This portrayal of the Lamb is meant to forever remind us that God's strength is made perfect in weakness. This truth is much neglected throughout Christianity. Too many Christians teach and preach with an emphasis on power and victory. Power and preeminence are wonderful, but the way to power is through death. Any power that has not been derived from the nature of the Lamb can very easily become corrupted.

Look at the state of the Church. See the corruption—moral corruption, ethical corruption and more. The lesson should be obvious: Do not reach for power. Lay your life down. Do not grab, give. Do not hold on to supremacy, because you will lose it. But whoever is willing to give it up will find it.

Some years ago, we had to counsel a dear brother who was in a position of leadership but who was having serious problems in his marriage. I remember saying to him, with love and concern, "Listen, if you hold on to your position, you'll lose it. But if you give it up, you'll find it."

Perhaps you have found yourself in a similar situation. You could hold on tightly; you could become very assertive; you could pray all kinds of "claiming" prayers. But hanging on so tightly guarantees that you will lose the very thing you value so much. Remember the words of Jesus: "Whosoever loves his life will lose it and whoever loses his life for My sake and the gospel's will find it" (see Mark 8:35 and John 12:25).

Jesus directed those words to His disciples, and you and I confess to being His disciples. Can we apply them to our own lives? (If the application of Scripture is not practical, it is not of God—because God is always practical.)

The Grace of Yielding

The Lamb who was slain shows us the way of surrender.

After my first wife died, I allied myself with four other Christian leaders and conducted a ministry as a single man. The five of us had committed ourselves not to make any major personal decisions without consulting one another, which was fine until a few years later when I fell madly in love with Ruth and wanted to ask her to become my wife.

I had just published a book called *The Grace of Yielding*, based on a message I had preached. The theme of the book was, "If you hold on, you will lose it; if you yield, you will keep it." I began to wish I had not preached that message or published that book, because when I submitted my marriage plan to the group, they said, "No." How could I lay down something I so dearly wanted? What was I to do? I believed that God was leading me to marry Ruth, but my brothers did not agree.

However, my own message convinced me that the right thing to do was to yield the whole situation to the Lord, and I did. Ruth and I could have gone ahead and gotten married without this exercise of yielding. But I do not believe we would have had the outpouring of God's blessing we received. Eventually the brothers agreed, and we were released to get married. Out of this incident, which was a major crisis in my life, came an extra abundance of provision and blessing from God.

Please let me ask you this question. Are you in some kind of situation where you may have rights you could easily claim? If you hold on to your claim, you will lose the outcome you desire. But if you yield it to God, you will be surprised at how much blessing will follow.

The grace of yielding is a good part of what it means to live and grow in the nature of the Lamb.

As we close this section of the book, it would be helpful to pause and think back over what you have read. Invite the Holy Spirit to highlight particular areas He desires to adjust in your life as you choose to cultivate the nature of the Lamb.

Lord Jesus, I have begun to see the beauty of Your character as the Lamb of God. It is so different from the way I have thought and acted. But I want to follow You more closely. Today I choose to yield to Your transforming process of purification. I ask You to make me ever more like You.

Holy Spirit, please help me to take on the nature of the Lamb and pour out Your grace so that I can make the right decisions every day. I humble myself in Your sight, seeking Your strength in my weakness and laying my life down at Your feet.

I pray this in Your precious name, Lord Jesus. Amen.

PART 3

CHOOSING *the* LAMB, EMPOWERED *by the* DOVE

In order to understand how to foster the nature of the Lamb in our lives, we must now turn our attention to the indispensable attributes of the Dove, otherwise known as the Holy Spirit.

In this final section of the book, we will start by examining the role of the Holy Spirit in the Old Testament. Then we will consider His activity in the family of John the Baptist, following that on into the New Testament. I will highlight two significant Spirit-experiences shown in the New Testament—the inbreathed Spirit (see John 20:22) and the outpoured Spirit, which happened for the first time on Pentecost (see Acts 2).

I want to make a distinction between regeneration and the baptism in the Spirit. To sum it up succinctly, I like to put it this way: Regeneration is the resurrected Christ, the inbreathed Spirit, received as life. Baptism in the Spirit is the glorified Christ, the outpoured Spirit, received as Lord. At that point, the Spirit becomes Lord in you.

Some people would say that the Word of God is entirely sufficient for us, and that we do not need so much emphasis on the Holy Spirit. My question is this: How can we truly understand God's Word if we do not open ourselves to the true interpretation of the Author, the Holy Spirit?

We know from John 1 that Jesus is the Word of God. But as we will discover in more detail, the Word needed the Spirit. The Holy Spirit descended on Jesus and remained on Him (see John 1:33–34). Jesus needed the Holy Spirit just as we do.

Having chosen to grow in expressing the nature of the Lamb, we have the wonderful expectation that the Dove will descend upon us and remain on us as we carry on in the Lamb's nature. This concluding part of the book will help us to explore what our life—with the empowering presence of the Holy Spirit—should look like.

15

THE HOLY SPIRIT IN THE OLD TESTAMENT

As we dig deeper into truths about God's Spirit—the Dove, who descends and remains on those who exhibit the Lamb's nature—let's begin with a quick outline of the manifestations or operations of the Holy Spirit in the Old Testament.

The Spirit and the Word

We are introduced to the Holy Spirit in the very first two verses of the Bible:

> In the beginning God created the heaven and the earth. And the earth was without form, and void; and darkness was upon the face of the deep. And the Spirit of God moved upon the face of the waters.
>
> Genesis 1:1–2 KJV

The Hebrew says the earth was *tohu va bohu*, which is an onomatopoeia meaning "in a mixed-up state." (Even when you pronounce the phrase, it sounds mixed up, similar to the phrase "topsy-turvy.")

In regard to the verb "moved" or "was moving," the actual Hebrew word means *a bird hovering*. So the Spirit of God hovered like a bird upon the face of the waters in the midst of chaos and darkness.

The next verse indicates how God's Word then went forth: "Then God said, 'Let there be light'; and there was light" (v. 3). Creation took place by the union of the Spirit of God and the Word of God. Together, these two sources brought the entire created universe into being. This is restated in one of the psalms: "By the word of the LORD the heavens were made, and all the host of them by the breath of His mouth" (Psalm 33:6).

Where the English translation says "breath," the Hebrew says "spirit" (*ruach*). So, it is by the Word and by the Spirit of the Lord that the universe was brought into being. The combined force behind all creation is God's Word and God's Spirit. Everything we have ever seen or will ever see springs from those creative sources: the Word and the Spirit of God.

We need to remember this truth, because whenever the Word and the Spirit of God are united in our own experience, the total creative power of God is again available to us.

Even at this very moment as you are reading this book, anything can happen, without limit—if the Word comes to you and the Spirit of God moves upon you. The entire creative ability of God is present when His Word and His Spirit unite. Learning how to engage in and respond to what God desires to do in our lives means that we can experience the creative power of His Word and His Spirit.

Bezalel

In the book of Exodus, we find another mention of the activity of the Holy Spirit. The Lord God was speaking to Moses:

See, I have called by name Bezalel the son of Uri, the son of Hur, of the tribe of Judah. And I have filled him with the Spirit of God [Bezalel was filled with the Holy Spirit of God], in wisdom, in understanding, in knowledge, and in all manner of workmanship [or craftsmanship], to design artistic works, to work in gold, in silver, in bronze, in cutting jewels for setting, in carving wood, and to work in all manner of workmanship.

Exodus 31:2–5

I am delighted by the fact that this manifestation of the fullness of the Holy Spirit in Bezalel was so very practical. One of the aspects of the Holy Spirit that I love is that He is always practical. (Anything that is not practical, in my opinion, is not truly spiritual.)

Bezalel was not filled with the Spirit of God so he could dream dreams or expound about abstract philosophical concepts. He was filled with the Spirit of God so he could become an exceptionally gifted artisan in gold, silver, bronze, precious stones and wood. Here was a man, Bezalel, whom God filled with the Holy Spirit for a specific purpose. Throughout the Bible we find that whenever God filled a person with the Holy Spirit, He did it for a purpose, intending to accomplish something specific through that person by His Spirit. Bezalel was intended to be the chief craftsman of the Tabernacle and its furnishings.

Joshua

Moving forward in the Old Testament, we come to the book of Deuteronomy, which refers to Joshua when he took over the leadership of Israel from Moses:

Now Joshua the son of Nun was full of the spirit of wisdom [that's one of the manifestations of the Holy Spirit—the

151

spirit of wisdom], for Moses had laid his hands on him; so the children of Israel heeded him, and did as the LORD had commanded Moses.

Deuteronomy 34:9

Please notice how Joshua came to be full of the spirit of wisdom: Moses laid his hands on him. Laying on of hands should not be an empty ritual. It should be an actual impartation of something significant from one person to another.

I suppose one of the greatest privileges God gives us is to impart spiritual gifts. Paul said to the Romans, "I long to see you, that I may impart to you some spiritual gift" (see Romans 1:11). In a certain sense, some spiritual gifts are indeed transferrable. This was what happened to Joshua as he was about to take over the difficult responsibilities of succeeding Moses. Thankfully, God made provision for the assignment. As the result of Moses laying his hands upon Joshua (just before the Lord took Moses away), Joshua was filled with the spirit of wisdom.

Gideon and the Judges

In the Old Testament book of Judges, we read the story of Gideon: "The Spirit of the LORD came upon Gideon; then he blew the trumpet, and the Abiezrites gathered behind him" (Judges 6:34). In the Hebrew, instead of "came upon" the word is "clothed": "the Spirit of the LORD *clothed* Gideon." It is a beautiful picture of being enveloped in the Holy Spirit as if a mantle were being wrapped around him. This seems to have been true for every one of the people recorded in the book of Judges who became the deliverers of Israel. Each was able to do what they did only by the Holy Spirit. Apart

152

from the Holy Spirit, they were just ordinary men (and one woman, Deborah).

For instance, we often think of Samson as a great giant of a man with bulging muscles. That may not necessarily have been the case at all. His strength was largely supernatural. No matter how big his muscles were, he could not have done what he did solely by his natural strength.

Thinking of Gideon, Charles Simpson once said, "Before you blow the trumpet, you had better be sure the Spirit of the Lord has come upon you." He was thinking also of King Saul, who blew his trumpet without the Spirit of the Lord upon him, and when the Philistines came out against him, he trembled. He had made the claims, but he did not have the qualifications.

With Gideon, however, it was different: "But the Spirit of the LORD came upon Gideon; then he blew the trumpet." If you "blow your trumpet" before the Spirit comes, you will waver and fall. If you wait until the Spirit comes upon you, you will be successful, as Gideon was.

The Lord took Gideon through several steps, and then He delivered complete victory into his hands.

King David

David did not attribute the psalms he wrote to his own genius or his own literary ability. He simply said, "I got it by the Holy Spirit. He gave me the words."

> Now these are the last [inspired] words of David.
>
> Thus says David the son of Jesse; thus says the man raised up on high, the anointed of the God of Jacob, and the sweet psalmist of Israel:
>
> ♥ "The Spirit of the LORD spoke by me, and His word was on my tongue."
>
> 2 Samuel 23:1–2

153

I suppose I have read most of the psalms at least two hundred times. As I read them each morning, I find myself saying, "I never read that verse before. I didn't even know it was there." I have also read the rest of my Bible consistently for many decades, and it continues to be more fresh and more surprising and more wonderful to me today than it was when I started. Why is that? Because it is not the product of natural reason, genius, talent, cleverness or artistic ability. Rather, it comes from the inexhaustible source of the Spirit of God.

"The Spirit of the LORD spoke by me, and His word was on my tongue." That was David's testimony. Previously, when David had sinned and bore terrible guilt before God as the leader of His people, this was his prayer, found in Psalm 51: "Do not cast me away from Your presence, and do not take Your Holy Spirit from me" (v. 11). David knew the one treasure he could not afford to lose was the presence of the Holy Spirit in his life.

In the late 1940s, there was a South African magazine called *The Standard Bearer*. I remember one particular issue I received at that time. The cover had a scene of a waterfall or something similar, with a sentence written below it that I have never forgotten: "Life's greatest tragedy is to lose the presence of God and not even know you've lost it." My inner response at that moment was, *God, may that never happen to me! May the Holy Spirit never leave me!*

Each of us can make David's prayer our own, even speaking it out loud right now: "Do not cast me away from Your presence, and do not take Your Holy Spirit from me."

The Prophets

The ministry of all the Old Testament prophets can be summed up in one verse: "For prophecy never came by the will of man, but holy men of God spoke as they were moved by the Holy Spirit" (2 Peter 1:21).

"As they were moved" could be translated from the original Greek, "as they were borne along by the Holy Spirit." I like the picture that phrase "borne along" conveys. The words of all true prophecy come to a prophet from the Holy Spirit, and "borne along" suggests a flow. A flow is never jerky, and neither is the flow of His inspiration. In fact, the flow of the Spirit is often compared to a flow of oil. Of all flowing substances, oil is probably the smoothest, without jerks and stops.

This chapter has been a very brief survey of the actions of the Holy Spirit (the Dove) that are recorded in the Old Testament. From before Creation and onward, the Holy Spirit has been present. He was responsible for Creation. He was responsible for the ministries of Moses, Bezalel, Joshua, Gideon, David and all the prophets. He continues to be responsible for countless specific actions today.

We must therefore reach the conclusion that anything God ever does on the earth is done through the instrumentality of His Holy Spirit. In the next chapter, we will take a look at the Holy Spirit in the lives of members of Zacharias's family just before God sent the long-awaited Messiah.

16

THE HOLY SPIRIT *INTO* THE NEW TESTAMENT

As we approach the advent of the Messiah, Jesus Christ, we find an increased emphasis on the Holy Spirit.

God set apart one remarkable family to prepare the way for the Messiah, the family of the priest Zacharias; his wife, Elizabeth; and their son—who became known as John the Baptist. We are told in the first chapter of Luke that every one of those persons was filled with the Holy Spirit.

This family was privileged to participate in the coming of the Messiah, and the word "Messiah"—*Meshiach* in Hebrew, *Christos* in Greek—means "the Anointed One," in other words, the One upon whom the Holy Spirit would rest. The very title "Christ" or "Messiah" indicates the presence and operation of the Holy Spirit. We do not have a Messiah if we do not have the Holy Spirit.

Zacharias and Elizabeth

The story of the preparation for the Messiah's coming begins in the first chapter of the gospel of Luke. An angel appeared to Zacharias in the Temple, and he was told that he and Elizabeth, who up to that point had been barren, would have a son. Zacharias was hesitant to believe such a statement, and he was rendered unable to speak until the boy was born.

The angel told him: "For he will be great in the sight of the Lord, and shall drink neither wine nor strong drink. He will also be filled with the Holy Spirit, even from his mother's womb" (Luke 1:15). That is to say, this little newborn baby, John, was already filled with the Holy Spirit, and he was "borne along" by the Spirit throughout his life.

Reading Luke's account, we next see Elizabeth, now carrying in her womb the unborn baby boy, when her cousin Mary comes to visit her—Mary, who is herself pregnant with the unborn Jesus. We read what occurred next:

> And it happened, when Elizabeth heard the greeting of Mary, that the babe leaped in her womb [that Spirit-filled baby, even in the womb, recognized the mother of the Messiah]; and Elizabeth was filled with the Holy Spirit. Then she spoke out with a loud voice and said: "Blessed are you among women, and blessed is the fruit of your womb!"
>
> Luke 1:41–42

℘ Speaking out boldly is one of the frequent results of being filled with the Holy Spirit. In almost every place where the New Testament reports people being filled with the Holy Spirit, the next words are, "they spoke" or "they prophesied"; they expressed something verbally.

This is what happened to Zacharias as well. Throughout Elizabeth's pregnancy, Zacharias had remained unable to speak, and he would write notes to communicate. Eight days after John was born, the time came to circumcise the baby boy, whom the people presumed was to be named after his father. Elizabeth objected, remarking that his name was supposed to be John, and they turned to the mute Zacharias for confirmation:

> And he asked for a writing tablet, and wrote, saying, "His name is John." So they all marveled. Immediately his mouth was opened and his tongue loosed, and he spoke, praising God. . . .
> Now his father Zacharias was filled with the Holy Spirit, and prophesied, saying:
> "Blessed is the Lord God of Israel . . ." [followed by a lengthy prophetic word].
>
> Luke 1:63–64, 67–68

Each of John's parents was filled with the Holy Spirit, as was John himself. Each prophesied. Each of their prophecies began with the word "Blessed." All of these Spirit-infused events formed part of the starting point for the actual coming of the Messiah.

The Messiah

In the first chapter of John, we read the words with which John the Baptist introduced the Messiah, the Christ. You will recall that John knew Jesus as his cousin, but he did not yet know Him as the Messiah. The whole purpose for John's ministry was to introduce and prepare the way for Jesus:

> "I did not know Him; but that He should be revealed to Israel, therefore I came baptizing with water."

And John bore witness, saying, "I saw the Spirit descending from heaven like a dove, and He remained upon Him. I did not know Him, but He who sent me to baptize with water said to me, 'Upon whom you see the Spirit descending, and remaining on Him, this is He who baptizes with the Holy Spirit.' And I have seen and testified that this is the Son of God."

John 1:31–34

These are very significant words. Not only were his words prophetic, but his acts were prophetic, as well. John's assignment was to baptize people in water. In effect, he was saying: "What you see me doing in water, the One who comes after me will do in the Holy Spirit." By these words, Jesus was introduced to Israel primarily as "the One who baptizes with the Holy Spirit."

Notice how interwoven everything is. Jesus could not be the Anointed One (the Messiah) unless the Holy Spirit had come down upon Him and remained upon Him. John could not have known any of this without being himself anointed by the Holy Spirit so that he could testify to having performed the actual baptism of Jesus as well as the visual evidence that He was truly the Son of God. As John also testified (see v. 29), Jesus is the Lamb of God who takes away the sin of the world—and it is His nature that we are called to emulate, which enables us to have victory over the Beast. But when we look at John's primary revelation of Jesus to the world while He was still on earth, it is as the One who baptizes in the Holy Spirit.

This statement by John the Baptist is found in all four gospels: Matthew 3:11, Mark 1:8, Luke 3:16 and John 1:33. How did God intend for Jesus to be presented to Israel? As "the One who baptizes with the Holy Spirit." Not primarily as the Savior; not primarily as the Lamb of God; but as the One who baptizes in the Holy Spirit.

How is it that for so many centuries most of the Church has hardly given any attention to this main aspect of Jesus' ministry? We are quite familiar with the statement about Jesus being the Lamb of God, which is His title found only in the book of Revelation and one of the four gospels. But we have not given as much weight to His designation as the One who baptizes in the Holy Spirit, found in all four gospels. In other words, this role is one of the most important truths we need to recognize about Jesus. As wonderful as it is to know Him as Savior and as the Lamb of God, that is not all He is. Every one of His disciples needs to come to know Him individually and personally as the One who baptizes in the Holy Spirit. I will teach further about this in chapter 21 and give you an opportunity to receive the Holy Spirit personally.

17

ASPECTS OF THE
HOLY SPIRIT

As the Dove (the Holy Spirit) descends on you and me and remains, enabling us to take on the nature of the Lamb, it is helpful to understand more about this "promise of the Father" (see Acts 1:4 and 2:33). In this chapter, I have assembled brief introductions to the primary aspects of the Holy Spirit as revealed in the Word of God.

The Person of the Holy Spirit

The first and most vital fact about the Holy Spirit is that He is a Person. Indeed, the Holy Spirit is an important Person, not just half a sentence at the end of the Apostles' Creed, which states: "I believe in the Holy Spirit. . . ." Probably one of the reasons we do not pay enough attention to Him is that He is so self-effacing; He never attracts attention to Himself. Rather He always focuses attention on and glorifies the Lord Jesus Christ.

When Jesus told His disciples that He was about to leave them, that He would withdraw from them so that He could return to His Father in heaven, He assured them that He had made provision for their well-being after His departure:

> Nevertheless I tell you the truth. It is to your advantage that I go away; for if I do not go away, the Helper will not come to you; but if I depart, I will send Him to you.
>
> John 16:7

> I still have many things to say to you, but you cannot bear them now. However, when He, the Spirit of truth, has come, He will guide you into all truth; for He will not speak on His own authority, but whatever He hears He will speak; and He will tell you things to come. He will glorify Me, for He will take of what is Mine and declare it to you.
>
> John 16:12–14

"Helper" could also be translated "Comforter" or "Counselor." The New Jerusalem Bible uses the word *paraclete*, which is a transliteration of a Greek verb probably best translated as "one called in alongside." Perhaps the closest equivalent would be "advocate," which has a legal connotation. In Britain we would call an advocate a "barrister"—someone who is called in alongside to help you plead your case in the law court when you are not competent to do it yourself.

All those words say something about the Holy Spirit. He is the Comforter, the Helper, the Counselor, the Paraclete, the Advocate. The Holy Spirit is a member of the Godhead, and He is a Person.

The disciples knew Jesus as a real Person, and He left them as a Person to return to the Person of the Father in heaven. But in His mission to bridge the gap between them and the

Godhead, He did not want to leave them alone and without resources. So He told His disciples, "When I return to heaven, I will send you another Person in my place." This underlines the Triune nature of God, one God in three persons: Father, Son and Holy Spirit. Each of those aspects of the Godhead is a Person. The Father is a Person, the Son is a Person, the Spirit is a Person.

When Jesus told His disciples, "It is to your advantage that I go away," they must have found that hard to accept. In essence, He was telling them, "You'll be better off with Me in heaven and the Holy Spirit on earth than you are with Me on earth and the Holy Spirit in heaven."

Many Christians say to themselves at one time or another, "Oh, wouldn't it have been wonderful to have been there during the days when Jesus was on earth, when we could actually fellowship with Him in His human form?" Yes, it would have been wonderful. But according to Jesus, we are much better off now with Jesus in heaven and the Holy Spirit on earth than any of us would have been if He were still on earth and the Spirit was still in heaven.

An exchange of Persons had to take place. One Person, Jesus, had to go away before the other Person, the Holy Spirit, could come.

Transformational Power

As the early Church grew, it became obvious that the Holy Spirit had brought radical transformation to the disciples of Jesus. When the Holy Spirit came on the Day of Pentecost (see Acts 2), the disciples of Jesus were transformed into new men and women in a way that none of them had been transformed the whole time Jesus was with them. Even up to their final moments with Jesus at the Last Supper, they were quarrelling among themselves as to which of them should be the greatest (see Luke 22:24–27).

What is more, they simply had not been able to understand even half of the profound truths about Jesus' death and resurrection. But as soon as the Holy Spirit came, they instantly gained a different grasp of Jesus' identity and of the meaning of His death and resurrection. They could put it all together—everything the Scriptures had predicted, as well as the statements their Teacher had uttered during their three years with Him.

Before the Day of Pentecost, Peter could never have stood up and applied the words of the prophet Joel to that situation. He would have had no insight. No amount of learning could have given him such lucidity and eloquence. The truths he preached on the Day of Pentecost could not possibly have come together in his head gradually—they came instantly. The moment the Holy Spirit came to the weary disciples in that upper room, their whole grasp of spiritual reality was revolutionized. A fisherman became a dynamic preacher and (as Jesus had predicted) a true "fisher of men."

The Pronoun "He"

We must not miss the fact that, in verse 13 of John 16 as quoted above, Jesus says, "However, when He, the Spirit of truth, has come, He will guide you into all truth." *He*, the Spirit of truth. *He* will guide you into all truth.

The Greek language in which the New Testament has come to us is a language that, like Spanish, French and others, designates genders for nouns—masculine, feminine and neuter. We have very little of that in English, although we have the three pronouns: he, she and it.

In the Greek language, the word for "spirit," *pneuma*, is neuter. It is neither masculine nor feminine. So the appropriate pronoun for Jesus to have used would have been *It*.

But in His statement in v. 13, He breaks the laws of grammar to use a different grammatical pronoun. Jesus does not say, "It will guide you"; He says *He*. Jesus wanted to leave no possible doubt that the Holy Spirit is unlike any other spirit, which would be just an "it." He is not just an influence. He is not just a doctrine. He is not a theological abstraction. He is a Person—and that is vital for us to know and remember.

If you and I fail to comprehend that truth, it will cause problems in relating to the Holy Spirit—just as I would have problems relating to my wife if I failed to recognize her as a person. I suppose that the uneasy relationship many people have with the Holy Spirit stems from their lack of understanding that the Holy Spirit is a Person.

There is more to consider regarding the Personhood of the Holy Spirit. Not only is He a Person, but He is *Lord*— just as much as God the Father is Lord and God the Son is Lord. God the Spirit is Lord. He is coequal with the other two members of the Godhead.

The Nicene Creed says of the Holy Spirit: "Who together with the Father and Son is worshiped and glorified." Worship belongs to God only, and the Holy Spirit is God and Lord.

In 2 Corinthians 3:17, Paul makes this simple statement: "Now the Lord is the Spirit; and where the Spirit of the Lord is, there is liberty." The use of "the Lord" in the New Testament corresponds to the use of the sacred name of God in the Old Testament, which is *Jehovah* or *Yahweh*. It is the name of the one true God. So, when Paul says, "The Lord is the Spirit," he is saying, "The Spirit is God; He is Lord." Then he adds, "Where the Spirit is, there is liberty."

Instead of being in bondage to a legal system, we have true liberty—wherever the Holy Spirit is. Somebody once paraphrased that verse to read like this: "Where the Holy Spirit is Lord, there is liberty."

Our liberty does not come from following a certain program in church on Sundays. It is not found in employing certain motions such as lifting up your hands, which can just as easily be bondage as liberty, depending on whether the Holy Spirit is prompting it or you are simply doing it out of religious tradition, habit or peer pressure. Religious traditions produce bondage. The Holy Spirit produces liberty.

Our Means of Access to God

When you and I begin to appreciate the Lordship of the Holy Spirit, we develop the same attitude of reverence toward the Holy Spirit that we have toward the Father and the Son. This is as it should be, because the only way for us to have access to God is by means of the Holy Spirit.

Here is a principle regarding the Godhead: The One who is sent as the representative has to be honored if one is to have access to the Godhead. When the Father sent the Son, He said, "From now on, no one comes to Me except through the Son" (see John 14:6). In other words, He was saying, "You cannot bypass My representative and come to Me. In every situation and circumstance, I uphold the One whom I have sent."

This, of course, is a theological issue, and I do not intend to enter into a deep theological discussion here. But we must understand that when Jesus had finished His task and returned to the Father, the Father and the Son sent the Holy Spirit. The same principle applies. You and I have no access to the Father and the Son except by the Spirit. We

166

cannot bypass the Spirit and come to the Father or to the Son. As Paul put it in his letter to the Ephesians: "Through Him [Jesus] we both [that is, both Jews and Gentiles] have access by one Spirit to the Father" (Ephesians 2:18).

You cannot leave out the Holy Spirit and have access. Many evangelical Christians focus on the fact that we have access to God through the Son, Jesus. That is perfectly true. But it is not the whole truth. Our access is through the Son by the Spirit to the Father. Likewise, the Father indwells us when we are in the Son through His Spirit (see John 14:23).

Whether you and I are going to God or whether God is coming to us, the Spirit is an absolutely essential part of the equation. We have access in the Son through the Spirit to the Father. The Father indwells us when we are in the Son through the Spirit. If we leave the Holy Spirit out of the equation, we have no access to God and God has no access to us.

We are totally dependent on the Holy Spirit.

Sensitivity to the Spirit

Someone has said, "The great sin of the Church for many centuries has been snubbing the Holy Spirit." We have not treated Him with the reverence, the honor or the respect to which He is due. I trust that the words I am sharing in this chapter will help to produce in your life the proper attitude toward the Holy Spirit.

In all successful relationships, *sensitivity* is imperative. Any married person would testify that when either partner in the relationship is insensitive to the other, the relationship suffers. Lack of sensitivity is probably the root cause in the breakdown of countless marriages. The same can be said of any close relationship. You cannot have a successful relationship with another person without mutual sensitivity.

My wife is a wonderful woman, but when she is under pressure—physical or emotional—she may at times speak with an uncharacteristic sharpness in her voice. She may be a little quicker to react, even prickly. At such times, what will happen if I get upset with what I consider to be an unreasonable attitude on her part? What if I react harshly to her response? What will be the result? I do not need to spell it out, do I? The result will be added friction and trouble in the relationship.

What is the problem? My lack of sensitivity to her situation. I should be able to discern when my wife is under pressure, and I should be extra tender and extra considerate at that moment in light of the pressure she is facing. But if I am blind to her situation or wrapped up in my own problems, I will not be sensitive enough. I might even complain, "Well, that's just like her to get temperamental just before I have to preach. She ought to have known better."

We need to bear this little comparison in mind as we relate to the Holy Spirit. You and I must be *sensitive* to the Holy Spirit. If instead we are thinking only of ourselves, our personal desires and our current problems, we will not relate rightly to the Holy Spirit.

Remember that the Holy Spirit is also the Dove, and doves are not only quiet and careful, but also sensitive and easily chased off. When you start to feel agitated or confused, stop and think about what you have been doing. There is always time to repent of taking matters into your own hands and failing to rely on the Holy Spirit. You need Him more than you realize.

18

JESUS AND THE
HOLY SPIRIT

Because the Dove chooses to rest and remain only on someone who exhibits the nature of the Lamb, you and I should learn how to cultivate and manifest the nature of the Lamb. Why? So that the Dove will settle and remain on us. Jesus attributed His whole ministry to the presence of the Holy Spirit. He never took credit for Himself for what He did. We will begin to see the same pattern in our lives as we choose to "walk just as He walked" (1 John 2:6).

In order to walk just as He walked, we must recognize the fact that the Holy Spirit directed everything Jesus did. Once when Jesus visited the synagogue in his home city, Nazareth, He chose to read aloud the prophecy of the prophet Isaiah, which described Him perfectly:

And He was handed the book of the prophet Isaiah. And when He had opened the book, He found the place where it was written:

169

"The Spirit of the LORD is upon Me,
Because He has anointed Me
To preach the gospel to the poor;
He has sent Me to heal the brokenhearted,
To proclaim liberty to the captives
And recovery of sight to the blind,
To set at liberty those who are oppressed;
To proclaim the acceptable year of the LORD."

Luke 4:17–19

John Wesley, quoting this passage in one of his journals, commented: "I suppose that these words are true of every man who has been truly called to proclaim the Gospel." Jesus could only live out such a message and ministry through total dependency on the Holy Spirit.

How can we more closely imitate His dependency on the Spirit? Only by means of the anointing of the Holy Spirit. If Jesus could not do it without the Holy Spirit, you and I can be very sure we will not be able to do it either. In a wonderful interaction, the Holy Spirit draws us to Jesus, transforms us increasingly into His image and continually helps us to stay the course.

In Isaiah 11:1–2, the prophet foreshows how the Holy Spirit was to set Jesus apart as the Messiah (the Anointed One). He lists seven distinct aspects of the Holy Spirit: the Spirit of the Lord (the Spirit that speaks in the first person as God), the Spirit of wisdom, the Spirit of understanding, the Spirit of counsel, the Spirit of might, the Spirit of knowledge and the Spirit of the fear of the Lord. When we are lacking in any of these important attributes, we receive them through the Holy Spirit.

But there is much more. The Spirit helps us worship. The Spirit guides us. The Spirit comforts us. The Spirit teaches us how to pray. The Spirit is a source of joy. The Spirit brings unity to the Body of Christ. The Spirit convicts us of sin so that we can repent—and even our repentance happens only with His aid. We could add many other influences the Spirit brings to us—in fact, the list is endless.

What Is the Dove Looking For?

We must then ask ourselves: What are some of the attitudes of our hearts and resulting conduct that attract the Dove—or repel Him? We should start by taking a look at our speech patterns, since our speech shows the condition of our hearts.

Paul wrote to the church in Ephesus about how *not* to speak:

Let no corrupt word proceed out of your mouth, but what is good for necessary edification, that it may impart grace to the hearers. And do not grieve the Holy Spirit of God [another way of saying "do not scare the Dove away"], by whom you were sealed for the day of redemption.

Let all bitterness, wrath, anger, clamor [shouting], and evil speaking be put away from you, with all malice.

Ephesians 4:29–31

More and more, I am becoming aware that even though my speech may not be vulgar or blasphemous, some of what I say is simply not very pleasing to the Holy Spirit, especially flippant words and expressions. Many people tell jokes that seem perfectly harmless. For example, people often tell "ethnic jokes" that make fun of certain nationalities or cultures. I have come to see that these may not be entirely pleasing to the Lord, because He loves all races and all nations. Also, we tend to use a lot of what the Bible calls "idle words." Jesus warned against them: "But I say to you that for every idle word men may speak, they will give account of it in the day of judgment" (Matthew 12:36).

As we mature in Christ and our hearts more closely resemble the Lamb's heart, our speech will reflect traits that will attract the Dove and cause Him to remain, such as tenderhearted kindness and forgiveness toward others. Throughout the New Testament epistles, we encounter basic behavior, such as, "Be kind to one another, tenderhearted, forgiving one another, even as God in Christ forgave you" (Ephesians 4:32).

Such traits come directly from the Spirit Himself, although we should note that there is a difference in kind between gifts and fruit. This may be illustrated by comparing a Christmas tree with an apple tree. A Christmas tree often carries gifts, and each gift is placed on or into its branches by a single act and received by a single act. No time or effort is required of the person receiving the gift.

On the other hand, both time and effort are required in order to cultivate an apple tree. To produce fruit, it must go through a series of stages that take years. First, the seed must be placed in the earth. From this a root goes down into the soil and at the same time a sprout rises upward. Over a period of years, the sprout grows into a tree. In due course blossoms appear on the tree. Then these fall off and fruit begins to develop. If the tree is to become strong, the blossoms or the young fruit must be plucked off in the first years so that the tree's root system will develop to support a strong tree. Several years must pass before the apples are fit to eat.

By means of this process, seed and fruit are inseparably linked to each other. Fruit must grow from a seed, but on the other hand, it takes fruit to produce further seeds. At the beginning of Creation, God ordained that every "fruit tree should yield fruit according to its kind, whose seed is in itself" (see Genesis 1:11). This establishes an important spiritual principle: Christians who do not produce spiritual fruit in their own lives have no seed to sow into the lives of others.

The New Testament speaks of spiritual fruit in the singular, while speaking of spiritual gifts in the plural. The nine forms of spiritual fruit (singular) can be found listed in Galatians 5:22–23: love, joy, peace, longsuffering (patience), kindness, goodness, faithfulness, gentleness and self-control. (Nine gifts are listed in 1 Corinthians 12:8–10: word of wisdom, word of knowledge, faith, healings, miracles, prophecy, discerning of spirits, tongues and interpretation of tongues.)

Love—the primary form of the fruit of the Spirit—is listed first in Galatians. The others that follow may be understood as different ways in which the fruit of love manifests itself.

Joy is love rejoicing.

Peace is love resting.

Longsuffering is love forbearing.

Kindness is love serving others.

Goodness is love seeking the best for others.

Faithfulness is love keeping its promises.

Gentleness is love ministering to the hurts of others.

Self-control is love in control.

We could also describe the fruit of the Spirit as the different ways in which the character of Jesus manifests itself through those whom He indwells. When all of the forms of fruit are fully developed, it is as if Jesus, by the Holy Spirit, is incarnated in His disciple.

The Dove is looking for these kinds of godly attributes in us, qualities that He Himself has implanted and nurtured.

When He sees them in us, He sees the nature of the Lamb. Then He will descend upon us and remain.

Union with Him

William Booth's daughter, Catherine Booth-Clibborn, who founded the Salvation Army in France, once said, "Christ loves us passionately and He wants to be loved passionately." While we nod in agreement with her, we nevertheless find that our relationship with Jesus often does not measure very high on the passion scale. Even though we see that the Bible reserves its most intense and passionate language for our human response to the Godhead, we know that our own words toward Him are not as heartfelt. What can we do about this?

We are aiming for a union with Christ Jesus that is even more passionate than the best marriage. In fact, Paul compares our union with the resurrected Christ to marriage: "Do you not know that your bodies are members of Christ? . . . He who is joined to the Lord is one spirit with Him" (1 Corinthians 6:15, 17).

What, then, is the ultimate function of the Holy Spirit? I believe it is to unite us with Christ, who died so that our human nature might be reckoned dead and so that we might have a reborn life in the Spirit. The Holy Spirit will enable our marriage union with the resurrected Christ—a union that is consummated by worship. Whenever we worship the resurrected Christ (as we are enabled to do by the Holy Spirit), we come into deeper union with Him. God seeks those who will worship Him in Spirit and in truth. As Jesus said: "God is Spirit, and those who worship Him must worship in spirit and truth" (John 4:24). The spirit of a believer is united with the Son of God through the Holy Spirit.

As we progressively cultivate the nature of the Lamb in our lives, the Dove enriches this union with the Lord until we become "one spirit with Him." We can scarcely conceive of that level of closeness. But that is what is offered to you and me as new creations, through the cross of Jesus and the work of the Holy Spirit in our lives.

The Word and the Spirit

We have touched briefly on Jesus and the Spirit, and now we turn our attention to the Word and the Spirit. This means that we will examine another side of Jesus—Jesus as the living Word of God.

The Word of God is not only the written Word (the Bible), because Jesus is the Word in person. We know this because of the way John introduces Him as "the Word" in his gospel:

> In the beginning was the Word, and the Word was with God, and the Word was God. . . . All things were made through Him, and without Him nothing was made that was made. In Him was life, and the life was the light of men. And the light shines in the darkness, and the darkness did not comprehend it. . . . As many as received Him, to them He gave the right to become children of God, to those who believe in His name: who were born, not of blood, nor of the will of the flesh, nor of the will of man, but of God. And the Word became flesh and dwelt among us, and we beheld His glory, the glory as of the only begotten of the Father, full of grace and truth.
>
> John 1:1, 3–5, 12–14

In other words, Jesus, the Lamb of God, is the personal Word of God. The Bible we hold so dearly is the written Word of God. Together, the truth of the written Word (the

Bible), the personal Word (Jesus, the embodiment of Truth) and the Holy Spirit (the Spirit of Truth) interact continually in three-part harmony. Keeping in mind the interplay of the Lamb (Jesus) and the Dove (the Spirit), let's review what we know about the written Word of God.

Author and Interpreter

First of all, we have to understand that the Bible has only one true Author—the Spirit of God. There were many human and angelic instruments involved in its composition, but only one Author who inspired it. Paul confirms this fact in one of his epistles to Timothy, where he writes, "All Scripture is given by inspiration of God" (2 Timothy 3:16).

This means that it was *inbreathed* by the Spirit of God. This is why all Scripture is authoritative and reliable. The prophets, kings and apostles who composed the words were all weak and fallible men. But with the Holy Spirit ruling over every aspect of its composition, preservation and compilation, the pure truth of God shines through its pages.

It is also very important to understand that the Holy Spirit is also the Interpreter of the Word. Wonderfully, the same One who authored the Scriptures will interpret them for us. (One could never seek a better interpreter for any book than the very author of that book.)

The Spirit will also help us remember the truth revealed in the pages of the written Word:

> But the Helper [Comforter, Counselor, Paraclete], the Holy Spirit, whom the Father will send in My name, He will teach you all things, and bring to your remembrance all things that I said to you.
>
> John 14:26

[The Spirit guides God's mature children (see Romans 8:14), at all times and under all circumstances, covering the past, the present and the future.] In Jesus' words: "When He, the Spirit of truth, has come, He will guide you into all truth" (John 16:13).

What a beautiful promise! After submitting to the leadership of the Holy Spirit, you and I do not need to worry about falling into error. When we cannot understand part of the written Word, we can rest in the fact that we belong to Someone who not only understands it, but who inspired it. "No prophecy of Scripture is of any private interpretation, for prophecy never came by the will of man, but holy men of God spoke as they were moved by the Holy Spirit" (2 Peter 1:20–21).

We may form our own conclusions about the interpretation of a prophecy, promise or passage of poetry in the Bible, but if we have not allowed the Holy Spirit to guide our thinking, our suppositions are not valid. Naturally we will find ourselves at different levels of interpretation at different times—remember the milk, bread and meat analogies in Scripture—but our core beliefs should be guided by the one Interpreter. He is indispensable; He has no substitute.

The physical Bible is finite, a volume with a certain number of pages, 66 books, a certain number of chapters, a certain number of verses, a beginning and an end. How can such a book meet our every need? How can it hold such an inexhaustible store of riches? Because it represents the mind and the heart of our infinite God.

The Lord gave me this analogy: A piano is an instrument, a piece of equipment. It has 88 keys, 52 of which are white and 36 of which are black. It has low notes, and it has high notes. Piano builders make them to clear specifications and then tune them to match a definite set of standards. But when a skilled pianist sits down at that instrument, the number of melodies he or she can produce is infinite. Limitless music can come out of that piano, that collection of finite parts, because of this one added factor—the interpreter, the player.

Who is the player on the "piano" of the Bible? The Holy Spirit. And we are the grateful listeners who are inspired to go on to action.

This means that when you read your Bible, the amount of insight you will receive from the Word of God will be proportional to the amount you open yourself to the Holy Spirit as you are reading. If you invite the Holy Spirit to assist you in reading and understanding Scripture, He is very willing to do so. But because He is never pushy or self-assertive, He almost always waits to be invited.

Having studied and read the Bible for over half a century, I must say that it is always becoming richer to me. It still seems new to me at every reading, and I am far from feeling that I have learned everything it can teach me. I approach the Scripture with anticipation, because I know truths are there just waiting for me to discover them. I know I will be instructed, encouraged and directed.

If you find reading the Bible to be something of a chore or a duty, why not ask the Lord right now to refresh your attitude toward His Word? Ask Him to open your spirit to His interpretation. Ask Him to show you gems of wisdom that you never saw before. You, too, can enjoy the written Word—and through reading it, you will allow the Spirit to mold you and shape you more into the nature of the Lamb.

19

PRAYER IN THE HOLY SPIRIT

L et's admit it. Without the help of the Holy Spirit, we cannot successfully live out any aspect of our new life in the Kingdom. Without Him, we cannot even appreciate our need for His help. Apart from Him, we are desperately limited and hopelessly weak. Apart from the involvement of the Holy Spirit, you and I cannot even pray a single effective prayer. We should find this reassuring:

> Likewise the Spirit also helps in our weaknesses. For we do not know what we should pray for as we ought, but the Spirit Himself makes intercession for us with groanings which cannot be uttered. Now He who searches the hearts knows what the mind of the Spirit is, because He [the Holy Spirit] makes intercession for the saints according to the will of God.
>
> Romans 8:26–27

We suffer from a twofold shortfall: We do not always know what to pray for, and even when we do know, we do not understand how to pray for it. No honest Christian would deny having those weaknesses. Good news: The Holy Spirit stands ready to help us in our weaknesses. The real secret of successful praying is "plugging in" to the Holy Spirit and letting Him pray through us. By this means, we can have a prayer meeting going on inside us 24 hours a day!

I am reminded of a story of a Swedish pastor who was traveling through his country. He visited a friend and spent the night in his home. At supper, the twelve-year-old son of his host began to express an interest in spiritual matters, and the pastor ended up praying for the young boy, who was baptized in the Holy Spirit and began to speak in tongues. At the end of the evening, the pastor went off to the guest room, and the father and son went off to another part of the house. They did not come together again until the next morning at breakfast.

At the breakfast table, the pastor asked his host, "How did you sleep?"

"Oh," he said, "I couldn't get any sleep last night. My son was speaking in tongues all night long!"

The pastor then asked the son, "And how did you sleep?"

"Oh," he said, "I slept perfectly." He had kept on praying in his new prayer language all night long, even while he was asleep, a bit like the young woman in the Song of Solomon: "I sleep, but my heart is awake" (Song of Solomon 5:2).

My first wife was like that. Lydia was a walking prayer meeting. She did not have to "get religious" to pray. She could be changing a baby's diaper and be praying at the same time. Lydia brought up a big adopted family in Jerusalem. The children would play "horses," riding on her back while she was praying, and that did not make any difference to her. She could be deep in prayer anywhere and anytime, even while she was standing at the stove, stirring the soup. For Lydia (as for any of us), prayer can be supernaturally natural—with the help of the Holy Spirit.

Four Kinds of Prayer

There are many different kinds of prayer, and I want to share a few of them with you. Please note that the Holy Spirit does not have just a few prayer methods in His repertoire. His inspiration is unlimited.

Prayer Based on God's Word

The Holy Spirit may speak to you or direct you to a promise in the Bible, and your prayer in such cases will be simple: "Lord, please do what You've said."

When Nathan the prophet brought a message to David that God was going to build a house (family line) for him, David went and sat in the presence of the Lord. (He did not kneel, apparently, and I am glad to see that. I think kneeling is just fine, but not when it makes us get so intense that we cannot allow the Holy Spirit simply to minister to us.) David sat and, I suppose, meditated on the tremendous promise God had just given him—something he had never even thought of asking for. After a time, David prayed: "Now, O LORD God, the word which You have spoken concerning Your servant and concerning his house, establish it forever and do as You have said" (2 Samuel 7:25).

That is one of the most powerful prayers you can ever pray: "God, You said it. You do it." Of course, you cannot randomly pick verses out of the Bible and say, "Okay, God, do this one for me." The Holy Spirit must lead you to the promise in Scripture. Once you have that revelation, you can pray with complete confidence, because you are no longer praying for only what *you* want, but for what *He* desires.

This truth immediately takes us back to the Lord's Prayer: "Your kingdom come. Your will be done on earth as it is in heaven" (Matthew 6:10 and Luke 11:2).

Mary, the mother of Jesus, shows us another great example of this kind of prayer. The angel Gabriel came to her (and remember, she was an unmarried virgin) with this tremendous message: "You are going to be the mother of the Son of God."

And Mary responded with these simple words: "Behold the maidservant of the Lord! Let it be to me according to your word" (Luke 1:38). That short prayer of assent released the greatest miracle in human history.

When you or I pray, "Let it be to me according to Your Word," we do not have to stomp our feet or shout or pray long prayers in theological language. Short and simple is much better when God Himself has shown you what He wants you to pray for.

Directly Inspired Prayer

In Psalm 81:10, we read this command from the Lord: "Open your mouth wide, and I will fill it." That simple advice can apply to prayer.

I will never forget the first public prayer I ever prayed. I was a soldier in the British Army, and I had received an invitation from a friend to attend a service at a Pentecostal church. I told my friend that I did not know what a Pentecostal was, and I had no idea what I was getting into, so I would go merely as a sightseer. At the service, a kindly, elderly couple who kept a boardinghouse saw these two hungry-looking soldiers and invited us home for supper after the service. (This became a critical turn in my whole life, because if dinner had not been offered, I probably would have just walked out of that church and never gone back.)

As we walked back to this couple's home, they were talking about the Bible as naturally as if they were talking about the news from the morning newspaper. They discussed everything as if it had just happened the day before—a phenomenon I simply could not understand.

When we arrived at their home, we immediately sat down at the supper table, a large oval table with seven or eight people seated around it, and someone prayed before we ate, which took me somewhat by surprise. I had never been any place where somebody prayed over food except for the Latin graces I had heard at boarding school. Then we enjoyed a delicious meal, and I was feeling satisfied that I had come.

However, at the end of the meal, they started to pray again without any warning or instruction. I quickly observed that they were praying by turns around the table, and I realized my turn was coming up soon. I was paralyzed with fear. I had never prayed a spontaneous prayer out loud in my entire life, and I had absolutely no idea what I was going to say.

But as in the verse we just read (even though I did not even know such a passage was in the Bible at that time), I opened my mouth wide and it got filled. I heard myself say these words: "Lord, I believe. Help my unbelief." After uttering those words, my mouth shut like a trap, and I could say no more. I may have never prayed a better prayer. You see, the Holy Spirit gave me that prayer in my weakness. In my desperation, He came to my help. I opened my mouth, and He filled it.

This is what you could call a directly inspired prayer. You do not compose it in your mind beforehand. You just open your mouth and let the Holy Spirit give you the prayer.

Supernatural Prayer

When my praying comes straight from my spirit, unfiltered by my mind, most often in a prayer language, or in

183

tongues, I call it supernatural prayer. Paul described it like this:

> For if I pray in a tongue, my spirit prays, but my understanding is unfruitful. What is the conclusion then? I will pray with the spirit, and I will also pray with the understanding. I will sing with the spirit, and I will also sing with the understanding.
>
> 1 Corinthians 14:14–15

Praying with the understanding means praying in my normal language, which, of course, I can comprehend. Praying with the spirit means praying in a language that the Holy Spirit has given me, but that I cannot understand. Praying with the Spirit is totally supernatural. Nobody can achieve it by his or her own effort. You may have studied six languages, but the Holy Spirit will give you a new one—one you have never heard before and never learned.

Every believer baptized in the Holy Spirit has the divine right and gift to communicate personally with the Lord in another tongue at any time. Paul wrote:

> For he who speaks in a tongue does not speak to men but to God, for no one understands him; however, in the spirit he speaks mysteries. . . . He who speaks in a tongue edifies himself, but he who prophesies edifies the church.
>
> 1 Corinthians 14:2, 4

There we have three functions or reasons for speaking in another tongue: (1) You are speaking to God, which is a tremendous privilege—direct communication spirit to Spirit; (2) you are speaking mysteries, secrets that you do not understand; (3) you are edifying or building yourself up.

Even if there were no other reasons, those would be sufficient, but there is more. The full gift of "varieties [kinds] of tongues" (see 1 Corinthians 12:28) goes beyond personal use. There are many different forms of tongues, which is a very rich field, including the following:

1. One kind of tongue is to speak a message out loud in the assembly in an unknown tongue that is to be followed by an interpretation.

2. Another use of tongues is as a sign to unbelievers. In my personal experience, this is very rare, but it happens at times when God's people are together or when God's people are ministering: A believer will speak a language that he does not know but an unbeliever present understands that language. This is actually what happened on the Day of Pentecost, when there were "devout men, from every nation under heaven" (Acts 2:5). And they were "confused, because everyone heard [the disciples] speak in his own language" (Acts 2:6).

3. It is not unusual to have the experience of increased intensity when you are speaking in tongues. It just comes out like a torrent, and it would seem that it occurs when confronting evil forces. You do not know how to pray and you do not know what to say, but the Holy Spirit comes through in tongues.

4. Tongues can also be simply for worship—communication with God.

Once at the end of a prayer gathering in Westminster Chapel in London, the pastor who had convened the meeting stood up to bring it to a close. As he was about to announce the final hymn, before he said anything in English, he spoke just a few short sentences in an unknown tongue. There was no interpretation and nothing more followed; the meeting was ended.

Not long afterward, I received a letter informing me what had happened with a guest couple at the meeting. The wife was a believer, but the husband was not. Apparently, this unbelieving husband had served with the army for some time on the northwest border of Pakistan (the southeast border of Afghanistan), and while there, he had learned the tribal dialect for that region. When the pastor had uttered those few short sentences in tongues, the husband had comprehended what the minister had said, because he had spoken in that tribal dialect. What the pastor had said was, "I am the Lord, and I am coming soon. Mark well, I am coming soon." Needless to say, this utterance had a profound effect on the man. Nobody can make such a thing happen; it is entirely supernatural.

Travailing Prayer

What I call travailing prayer is a different kind of prayer. This can be a groaning, even somewhat inarticulate, way of praying. Paul described it in one of his letters:

> For we know that the whole creation groans and labors with birth pangs together until now. Not only that, but we also who have the firstfruits of the Spirit, even we ourselves groan within ourselves, eagerly waiting for the adoption, the redemption of our body.
>
> Romans 8:22–23

Truly this is Spirit-formed prayer, and it flows through us as we allow the Holy Spirit to express Himself. Paul goes on to explain:

In the same way, the Spirit helps us in our weakness. We do not know what we ought to pray for, but the Spirit himself intercedes for us through wordless groans. And he who searches our hearts knows the mind of the Spirit, because the Spirit intercedes for God's people in accordance with the will of God.

Romans 8:26–27 NIV

I once read an account of the great 1904 Welsh revival. A man named Evan Roberts and his older brother were very much used by the Spirit as leaders in that move of God. These brothers had come from a comparatively poor family in Wales, and they had shared the same bed together for many years. Evan Roberts's brother reported that for many months before the revival broke out, Evan would lie in bed each night asleep, his body shaking with great groans and sobs. Evan himself was not aware of the shakings and groanings that were happening to him as he slept. After a time, the revival broke loose. I believe that it was brought about in large part by those intercessory groans, and that they also had much to do with the role that Evan Roberts was later to play in that revival.

A Symphony of Prayer

There are as many different kinds of prayer as there are instruments in an orchestra. If all Christians were engaged in Spirit-directed prayer, God would hear a whole orchestra praying (playing). Individuals would be playing the piccolo or the clarinet, the violin or the cello. Others would be sounding the timpani to the Conductor's baton—all together it would be a whole symphony orchestra of prayer. There is nothing dull, regimented or stereotypical about such a wide-ranging variety of prayer, offered up under the skillful direction of the Holy Spirit.

20

IMMERSION IN THE HOLY SPIRIT

I have taught about the baptism in the Holy Spirit throughout my years of ministry, and I have been privileged to
pray for countless believers to receive it. In this book, I
have been highlighting the significance of our relationship
with God's Holy Spirit, as well as the need to cultivate the
nature of the Lamb in a way that allows the Holy Spirit to
remain upon us. However, He cannot remain if we have never
received Him or if He has never been poured out upon us!

One of the primary revelations of Jesus recorded in all
four of the gospels is that He would be the "Baptizer in the
Holy Spirit" (see Matthew 3:11, Mark 1:8, Luke 3:16, John
1:33). After His earthly ministry was completed, following
His resurrection, Jesus repeated this promise of baptizing
with the Holy Spirit: It is important to emphasize how frequently this promise is given in the gospels. Acts 1:4–5 records what Jesus said to His disciples:

> And being assembled together with them, He commanded
> them not to depart from Jerusalem, but to wait for the Prom-

ise of the Father, "which," He said, "you have heard from Me; for John truly baptized with water, but you shall be baptized with the Holy Spirit not many days from now."

Acts 1:4–5

The fulfillment of this promise of Jesus is recorded in Acts 2:1–4 on the Day of Pentecost. Let's read what the Bible says in that passage, and then briefly consider exactly what is implied:

When the Day of Pentecost had fully come, they were all with one accord in one place. And suddenly there came a sound from heaven, as of a rushing mighty wind, and it filled the whole house where they were sitting. Then there appeared to them divided tongues, as of fire, and one sat upon each of them. And they were all filled with the Holy Spirit and began to speak with other tongues [or other languages], as the Spirit gave them utterance.

KEY !

I see three successive features of this experience. First there was a *baptism*. The Holy Spirit came from above and immersed them. It filled the whole house where they were sitting. They were immersed from above.

Second, there was a filling. Each of them was *individually filled* with the Holy Spirit. It was not just a collective experience. It was an experience in which each individual had his or her own personal share.

Third, there was an overflow—a *supernatural outflow* from the infilling, along the lines of the principle Jesus had stated earlier: "Out of the abundance of the heart the mouth speaks" (Matthew 12:34). When your heart is filled, it overflows through the mouth in speech. Throughout the New Testament when we see people being filled with the Holy

Spirit, they spoke a word or a message, prophesied or spoke out in tongues.

People are obliged to cooperate with God's Spirit. He fills them, but *they* must open their mouths and speak. The Holy Spirit does not do the speaking; they do, as the Holy Spirit gives them the language.

The Holy Spirit: A Seal, a Deposit and a Guarantee

The apostle Paul describes this experience using contractual terms:

> Now it is God who makes both us and you stand firm in Christ. He anointed us, set his seal of ownership on us, and put his Spirit in our hearts as a deposit, guaranteeing what is to come.
>
> 2 Corinthians 1:21–22 NIV

> You also were included in Christ when you heard the message of truth, the gospel of your salvation. When you believed, you were marked in him with a seal, the promised Holy Spirit, who is a deposit guaranteeing our inheritance until the redemption of those who are God's possession—to the praise of his glory.
>
> Ephesians 1:13–14 NIV

The Holy Spirit is a seal and a deposit, a guarantee or down payment of our inheritance in Christ Jesus. The Spirit marks us publicly in order to set us apart. In days gone by, you would send a piece of registered mail by sealing it with hot wax and then putting an imprint on it. The Holy Spirit seals us like that.

Many years ago, my first wife, Lydia, and I were shopping in the market in Jerusalem for curtain material. We found what we wanted and paid the *eravon*—the Hebrew word for guarantee. That payment was a deposit or down payment and guaranteed that the material would be held in reserve for us. It was also an assurance that we would be coming back with the rest of the payment to take what we had reserved.

As a deposit, the Holy Spirit is likewise a guarantee from Jesus. By granting us this experience, Jesus says, "I'm coming back to take you. When I return, I'll come back with the rest of the payment. Then you will be Mine forever." These three words—seal, deposit, guarantee—provide a clear picture of what the baptism in the Holy Spirit is.

What exactly is the seal we receive? People debate this question, but as far as I am concerned, the New Testament indicates only the seal of speaking with other tongues, as given by the Holy Spirit.

I am aware that there are cults (the Rastafarians in Jamaica, for one) in which people speak in tongues. This frightens some people, who worry, *How do I know I'm going to get the right thing?* Jesus promised us that if any child of God asks the heavenly Father for a piece of bread, He will not give that person a stone. If he or she asks for a fish, He will not give a serpent (see Matthew 7:9–11 and Luke 11:11). In other words, you do not need to be afraid. If you are a child of God and you ask for the Holy Spirit, He will give Him to you. If you are not a child of God, the promise does not apply.

By definition, a seal must be something visible, something audible, something public. A secret seal cannot accomplish its purpose. The seal of the Holy Spirit was the seal the apostles themselves received; Jesus told them to wait in Jerusalem until they received the Father's promise. They did. When the Holy Spirit came, the disciples spoke with tongues. After that experience, they did not need to wait anymore.

191

This was the same seal they subsequently accepted in others. They never asked for any other seal. Many people have asked me, "Brother Prince, how do I know if I've been baptized in the Holy Spirit? I've had various experiences as I have been praying and seeking God. But how can I know?" I always answer: You will know when you receive the seal. When you first begin to speak with other tongues as the Spirit gives you to speak, you will know you have been baptized in the Holy Spirit.

To repeat: The New Testament does not offer us any other seal. Therefore, as strange and offensive as the baptism in the Spirit may seem—some misguided people even call it demonic—this is the seal God has designated. I have learned that God sometimes puts a kind of stumbling block in the way, so that a person who is not really in earnest will be put off. The seal of speaking in tongues can be like that. Do you want to receive the fullness of the Spirit? Then accept it with both hands.

From the Scriptures, as well as from personal experience, I can see two ways that the Holy Spirit comes to people: (1) directly from heaven, falling on people; this was what happened on the Day of Pentecost and in the house of Cornelius (see Acts 2 and 10); (2) by the laying on of hands (see, for example, Acts 8:14–19). Baptism with water was a separate experience, coming sometimes before and sometimes afterward.

Purposes of the Baptism in the Holy Spirit

I would identify three primary purposes for the baptism in the Holy Spirit:

1. Power to witness
2. Power to perform signs and wonders
3. Unity

The overall purpose of the baptism in the Holy Spirit is to receive supernatural power from God. This is how Jesus Himself explained it to His disciples just before He ascended into heaven. These are His last recorded words on earth: "But you shall receive *power* when the Holy Spirit has come upon you; and you shall be witnesses to Me in Jerusalem, and in all Judea and Samaria, and to the end of the earth" (Acts 1:8, emphasis added). The word for "power" there in Greek is *dunamis*, from which we get the English word "dynamite." As we all know, dynamite causes explosions. You will aptly observe that when the Holy Spirit descended on the Day of Pentecost, an explosion took place.

Many Christians say the disciples had already been empowered by the fact that Jesus had risen from the dead. But that is not accurate. Jesus had risen from the dead fifty days earlier, and no one in Jerusalem had heard about it. But when the Holy Spirit came, all Jerusalem heard about it in a few hours. Suddenly, they had received the power to be bold and effective witnesses.

The message of the Gospel is itself supernatural. It is not a record of natural events, but rather something totally supernatural. Jesus died, was buried, rose from the dead and ascended into heaven. All of that is supernatural. If you and I are going to testify to supernatural events of this type, we need supernatural power. Just a grasp of theology is not enough. We need to be *empowered*.

By the power of the Holy Spirit, the message we proclaim will be supported by supernatural signs and wonders. Paul described his own ministry:

> I will not dare to speak of any of those things which Christ has not accomplished through me, in word and deed, to

make the Gentiles obedient—in mighty signs and wonders, by the power of the Spirit of God.

Romans 15:18–19

We see a similar testimony in Hebrews 2:3–4:

> How shall we escape if we neglect so great a salvation, which at the first began to be spoken by the Lord, and was confirmed to us by those who heard Him, God also bearing witness both with signs and wonders, with various miracles, and gifts of the Holy Spirit, according to His own will?

The unbelieving world has a right to expect miraculous signs from the Church. This is what we should be supplying by the power of the Spirit. If we just present an intellectual message and quote a few Scriptures, we are operating at a level below the will of God. Some people will get saved, which is wonderful. But it is not adequate for the task of evangelizing the whole world. We need *dunamis*! One and all, we need to be baptized in the Holy Spirit.

This brings us to a discussion of that little word, "in." First Corinthians 12:13 may be one of the most misunderstood verses in the New Testament, because the Bible translators (who, I would argue, had a preconception of what Paul was trying to say), substituted the word "by," where the Greek word means "in": "For by one Spirit we were all baptized into one body—whether Jews or Greeks, whether slaves or free—and have all been made to drink into one Spirit."

The Greek says *in* one Spirit we were all baptized *into* one body. There is no suggestion anywhere else in the New Testament that the Holy Spirit ever baptizes people. People are baptized *in* the Holy Spirit, not *by* Him.

194

People are baptized *in* something and *into* something, as in the case of John's water baptism and Christian water baptism. John's baptism was a baptism of repentance, but he would not baptize people who had not repented. His baptism did not produce repentance; it was the acknowledgment that they had already repented. With Christian water baptism, we are baptized into Christ. When we are baptized, we are already in Christ; otherwise we have no right to be baptized. Being baptized in water publicly designates us as already having been in Christ.

The purpose of being baptized in the Holy Spirit is so that we can come into unity as a body. Look at the emphasis on the word *one*: "For by [or in] one Spirit we were all baptized into one body . . . and have all been made to drink into one Spirit."

In one Spirit, we were all baptized *into* one body. I am not suggesting that we are only made part of the Body of Christ when we are baptized in the Holy Spirit, but that this is the *seal* that we are in the Body. If we were to show this in a simple table, it would look like this:

Type of Baptism	In What?	Into What?
John's baptism	Water	Repentance
Christian baptism	Water	Jesus Christ
Baptism in the Holy Spirit	Holy Spirit	One Body (the Church)

One of the tragedies of Church history is that instead of producing unity, the baptism in the Holy Spirit has sparked division. Instead of accepting our unity in the Holy Spirit, we Christians have too often allowed our stance on the Holy Spirit to produce division. For that, all of us need to repent.

The Holy Spirit baptism is designed to show us that we are part of one Body. We should allow the Spirit to convince us that every other true believer, no matter what denomination or race or culture, is a fellow member of the same Body. There is only one Body, and there is only one Holy Spirit. Let's surrender ourselves anew to His guiding and transforming influence.

21

RECEIVING
THE HOLY SPIRIT

In my opinion, most Christians are living bottled-up lives. They do not possess the freedom to express what God has put into them because of perceived standards of dignity: "Always speak with a quiet voice." "Do not get too excited." "Sit calmly and upright in your pew." "Stand up, sit down and kneel at all the proper times." "Shake the hand of the preacher as you exit the church." You know what I mean.

What I have just described has very little in common with the experiences of people in the Bible. They got excited. They made noise. Read the psalms of David and you will see that he cried, he roared, he drenched his bed with his tears. He was a man of strong emotion. Even Jesus Himself showed great emotion. He groaned. He wept. He zealously overturned the money changers' tables. He expressed His feelings. When the apostle John encountered the risen Jesus in the book of Revelation, he fell at His feet like a dead man; Jesus' supernatural power overwhelmed him.

What is the trouble with us? We have suppressed our emotions. We do not give free expression to what God is doing in us. We have quenched the Spirit, making it our aim to be dignified above all else. We have been guided by fears of becoming too emotional or too excited. As you may know, I have never been a very emotional person. But I do believe in *yielding* to the Holy Spirit. I believe in freely expressing what the Holy Spirit has put in me.

Were the apostles all very dignified on the Day of Pentecost when the Holy Spirit came? No! Just the opposite. They behaved in a very strange, undignified way. They all raised their voices at the same time, speaking in a cacophony of languages they had never learned. It was so over-the-top that the crowd of unbelievers said, "They're drunk!" (Has anyone ever said that about you as you were walking out of church?)

Such physical manifestations are part of the package—and we should accept them without fear or hesitation. It is part of our yielding to Him our control of everything in our lives. Once we determine to cooperate with Him in every way, we can much more freely step into the fullness of the Spirit.

Besides being willing to be a "fool for Christ," I have identified seven prerequisites or requirements for receiving the Holy Spirit. They are as follows:

1. **Repent.** "Repent, and be baptized" (Acts 2:38).
2. **Be baptized in water.** The full promise is, "Repent, and be baptized, and you *will* receive the Holy Spirit" (see Acts 2:38). (In my opinion, we should be baptized just as Jesus was, by full immersion.)
3. **Be thirsty.** Jesus said, "If anyone thirsts, let him come to Me and drink" (John 7:37).

4. **Come to Jesus.** There is only one Baptizer in the Holy Spirit, and you have to come to Him to be baptized in the Spirit.

5. **Ask.** Do not assume that He will simply give you the Spirit without your specific request. Jesus said, "If you then, being evil, know how to give good gifts to your children, how much more will your heavenly Father give the Holy Spirit to those who ask Him!" (Luke 11:13).

6. **Receive.** Receiving is like drinking or breathing in (see John 20:22).

7. **Yield your tongue.** This is the hardest step for some people. The Bible portrays the tongue as the most "unruly" member of your body—you cannot control it on your own. Yielding the use of your tongue to the Holy Spirit provides one of the best evidences that the Lord has come in to take control. (Do not worry that you will open a vocal torrent that you cannot shut off; you will remain in control over starting and stopping.)

In parts of the Bible, the tongue is called "my glory." This does not come out in all translations, but in Psalm 16:9, the psalmist said, "Therefore my heart is glad, and my glory rejoices." When Peter quoted that passage in Acts 2:26, he said, "Therefore my heart rejoiced, and my tongue was glad." Did you know that your tongue is your "glory" because it was designed for that one supreme purpose—to glorify God? Any use of the tongue that does not glorify God is a misuse. But when the Holy Spirit takes control of your tongue, everything He uses your tongue for will glorify God.

Even if you may not have met the seven basic conditions above in chronological order, the Holy Spirit will come to you. For instance, you may not yet have been baptized by full immersion in water—as I was not. In fact, I did not even know yet about being baptized.

When I was baptized in the Holy Spirit, I first noticed a strange sensation in my belly, and I thought, *What's this?* Then an unusual phrase came to my mind: "speaking with other tongues." I thought, *What has this feeling in my belly got to do with speaking with other tongues?* Then I said out loud in that empty room: "God, if You want me to speak with tongues, I'm ready to do it." The feeling in my belly moved up through my chest and into my throat, and my tongue started to move. I was not controlling it, nor did I try to. The next thing I knew, I was speaking a language like Chinese. I had not really asked, and I had not yet been baptized in water. I took care of that later. The One who baptizes in the Spirit had met me where I was.

Thirsty?

Are you getting thirsty yet? I hope so. Then you can come to Him and have your thirst quenched, and as Jesus promised, wonderful things will happen inside you:

> On the last day, that great day of the feast, Jesus stood and cried out, saying, "If anyone thirsts, let him come to Me and drink. He who believes in Me, as the Scripture has said, out of his heart [the King James Version says "belly"] will flow rivers of living water." But this He spoke concerning the Spirit, whom those believing in Him would receive; for the Holy Spirit was not yet given, because Jesus was not yet glorified.
>
> John 7:37–39

The Holy Spirit could not be given until Jesus was glorified. But now that He has taken His rightful place at the Father's right hand, any of us can receive His Holy Spirit. What a marvelous transformation! You come to Him parched and thirsty, and instantly you become a channel for rivers of living water. How does it happen? Very simply: You come to Jesus, the only Baptizer. You come to the Baptizer to drink in the baptism of the Holy Spirit.

Some religious people have a problem with this. It seems too simple to be true, and they fail to open their hearts and mouths. Yet how can you drink with your mouth closed? You cannot. You drink by opening your mouth and taking something in, in this case the supernatural power of God.

I have seen as many as three thousand people at the same time receive the Holy Spirit. Every one of them drank in the Spirit, and after the drinking, there was an overflow. We cited the Scripture "out of the abundance of the heart the mouth speaks" (Matthew 12:34), and that is what happened. They had faith that the Lord would quench their thirst—and they opened their mouths, not only to drink but to speak forth as the Holy Spirit gave them the words.

Receive Him Now

If you would like, you can pray the simple prayer below to receive this wonderful, supernatural experience. You can present yourself to Jesus, ask to be baptized in the Holy Spirit and then drink. We do not receive the Holy Spirit by praying; we receive Him by drinking.

First, confess your faith in Jesus as your Savior. (If you have never been saved, you can be saved right now as you pray this prayer.) At the end of the prayer, after you say, "Amen," do not pray anymore in English. Remember that when you are speaking your own language, you cannot speak another. You must stop speaking English in order to begin to speak the new language.

Please pray this very simple prayer. Then begin to drink and speak out of the overflow.

Lord Jesus Christ, I believe that You are the Son of God and the only way to God. I believe that You died on the cross for my sins and rose again from the dead. I confess the sins I have committed, and I trust You to forgive me and to cleanse me by means of the blood You shed on the cross. I thank You for doing this.

Now, Lord Jesus, I come to You as my Baptizer in the Holy Spirit. I open myself up to You and I begin to drink of Your Spirit, which You are already pouring out on me. I trust You, Lord, to give me so much to drink that it overflows. In faith I thank You! I pray this in the name of Jesus. Amen.

Now begin to drink. Just open your mouth, drink in, yield your tongue and begin to speak. You do not have to shout, but you need to speak clearly enough to know you have said it. Just take time to enjoy the Lord. Forget your problems. Forget your questions. Just let yourself go. Release yourself to the Lord through this experience.

If you feel like laughing, go ahead; it is perfectly scriptural. Psalm 126:2 speaks of the Lord filling our mouths with laughter and our tongues with shouts of joy. You do not have to hold back.

Forget your dignity and get excited. Jesus did not say "puddles of living water"—He said *rivers* (see John 7:38). Let it flow. Do not cut it off. Freely bask in the knowledge that you are now praising the Lord in a language you never learned. Do not quit until you have absolutely no doubt that the Lord has given you this gift. Go on thanking Him in the language He has given you.

Having just prayed in a language you have not learned, now take a moment to thank Him in English again:

Thank You, Lord Jesus. You are worthy. Worthy is the Lamb that was slain to receive glory and honor and power and blessing. Hallelujah! I love You, Lord Jesus, and I'm not ashamed to tell You. I love You because You first loved me. Thank You for what You have done in my life just now, Lord. I give You all the glory and all the praise because it is due to You alone. Amen.

22

LED BY THE SPIRIT

I trust that with the help of what was shared in our previous chapter, you were able to enter into the wonderful experience of receiving the baptism in the Holy Spirit and speaking with tongues. If for some reason you have not yet received, I would encourage you to go back over the last chapter. As you are reading, ask the Lord to show you if there is anything hindering you. Remember that all gifts of the Spirit are received by faith, so don't fall into the trap of doubt, fear or unbelief. It could be a simple matter of a sin He wants to bring to your remembrance so that you can ask forgiveness and receive His mercy. The Lord is faithful, and if you keep asking and following His lead, you will receive what you ask for.

Following His lead is what this chapter is about. What does this new life in the Spirit look like, practically speaking? How does your new life in the Spirit enable you to cultivate the nature of the Lamb?

We have already covered numerous aspects of the life of faith. We recognize that, contrary to the "beastly" ambition and aggression we see in the world around us, we are called to lay down our lives in meekness and purity. We have discussed the importance of manifesting the nature of the Lamb so that the Dove (the Spirit) will settle and remain on us.

How can we learn to let the Dove, the Holy Spirit, lead us in day-to-day life? In my experience, very few Christians have ever had proper instruction on this extremely important topic.

An inability to follow the leadership of the Spirit is clearly one of the root problems of the Church. Generations of Christians who have been born again have never been taught how to be led by the Spirit. They enter the Kingdom of God, only to stumble around for the rest of their earthly lives, never making any real progress toward maturity.

No Substitute

The Holy Spirit is absolutely unique. He can do what no other person and no other power can do. The Dove is the only One who can accomplish the will of God in a human life. "Not by might nor by power, but by My Spirit," said the Lord of hosts to Zerubbabel, the governor of Judea, after the people returned from the Babylonian exile (Zechariah 4:6). The "Lord of hosts" is the Commander of all of the forces of heaven and earth. Even so, He says, "It will not be accomplished by the mighty power of My heavenly armies, but solely by My Holy Spirit."

Simply put, no amount of force can do what has to be done—which is to *change people inside*, radically, so they can be united with God. No exertion of peer pressure can do that, and no amount of human effort. Education will not work. Talent is not enough. Law enforcement cannot do it. Money cannot buy it.

Only one Agent can transform human hearts and renew human thinking while also furnishing the sustaining strength to enable us (individually and together) to fulfill His purposes. If you want to enter into the life the Lord has prepared for you in Christ, *you must be completely dependent upon the Holy Spirit*. There is no substitute.

No Other Way to Mature

When you were reborn of the Spirit of God, you became a child of God. The Greek word for "child" is *teknon*. But Paul did not use that word when he wrote, "For as many as are led by the Spirit of God, these are sons of God" (Romans 8:14). Where we see "sons," Paul did not use the word for babies, but rather the word for mature sons and daughters. That Greek word is *huios* ("mature sons"). Paul is saying that the only people who qualify to be mature sons and daughters of God are those who have been *led by the Holy Spirit*.

The verb in Romans 8:14 is in the continuing present tense in Greek: ". . . as many as are [being continually] led by the Spirit of God." This is not something that happens only in church on Sunday morning or when you kneel by your bed to pray. It is something that happens day by day, hour by hour, moment by moment. That is how maturing works. Absolutely the only way to grow to maturity as a child of God is to be continually led by the Holy Spirit of God.

The maturation process will always vary from one person to the next—it is perfectly personalized for each of us. I had a tremendously powerful personal experience of the Holy Spirit. When I first came to know Jesus as a young British soldier, I ended up on the floor of my barracks room under the power of God for well over an hour. My initial encounter with Jesus was also an encounter with the Holy Spirit and His power. From then on, the Holy Spirit was always a reality to me.

I believed in the Holy Spirit, and I went on to study about the Holy Spirit. When I became a preacher, I preached about the Holy Spirit, preaching many, many times about how a person must be born again of the Spirit. But looking back now, I have to say with regret that for me at that time, the Holy Spirit was rather like an emergency vehicle. Whenever I was in desperate trouble, I phoned for the ambulance. The ambulance always turned up and helped me. But that made for a very spasmodic relationship with the Holy Spirit.

Instead of being immersed in the Spirit, I seemed to be more deeply immersed in religion. Eventually I found out that religion and the Holy Spirit do not very often get along well together. Being busy with religious exercises and activities makes us tend to rely on those automatically instead of relying on the Holy Spirit. Back then, I used a lot of spiritual language, but my life lacked much real spiritual content. Over time, sparing you the details, I will simply say that the Lord took me through various experiences one after the other, all of which were designed to make me aware of my total dependence on the Holy Spirit.

Perhaps you have been going through frustrations, problems and heartaches. You may have asked, "Why are You taking me through this, Lord?" From my own experience, I will offer one very likely reason why the Lord has permitted these problems to come into your life—to show you that you need the Holy Spirit every day, every hour and every moment, and to teach you how to rely on Him. There is no other way to succeed in the Christian life than to be led by the Holy Spirit.

One especially encouraging truth about the Holy Spirit is that He is always willing to lead us. We never have to coerce

Him or cajole Him to help us. The problem, if there is a problem in the Leader-follower relationship, will always lie with us, never with the Holy Spirit.

The reason you and I function well only intermittently is because, as Scripture tells us, "The flesh lusts against the Spirit, and the Spirit against the flesh; and these are contrary to one another, so that you do not do the things that you wish" (Galatians 5:17). Our old carnal nature (which follows the nature of the wild Beast) carries a built-in antipathy toward the Spirit. Thus, we must learn to set it aside, reckoning it dead through the death of Jesus on the cross. Only then can we live for the Lord through the Spirit. We have to learn not to allow our carnal nature to dictate the terms.

This is not an instantaneous experience. Nobody acquires a lamb nature overnight. Some people—and they are usually the conspicuously successful Christians—do learn it quickly. They are not necessarily preachers. Often, they are just regular people who are faithful members of the Body of Christ. Very often, the intercessors, the people who pray in secret and who cultivate a close relationship with God, seem to learn this lesson first.

The lesson, however long or short the schooling process may be, is the same: The Holy Spirit is essential for this process of maturity, and there is no other option.

What the Holy Spirit Is Seeking

Scripture reveals a beautiful picture of the attitude the Holy Spirit is looking for in a person. Initially, He found it in only one man—Jesus. We know that the Dove descended upon Him in bodily form. But that was not the most significant fact. The most telling piece of evidence that Jesus was the Lamb was that the Holy Spirit *remained* on Him.

Even though the Holy Spirit has descended upon many of us as well, all of us have said or done things that have scared the Dove away. Jesus never scared the Dove away. His behavior and His very nature were entirely united to the nature of the Godhead. He was, in fact, the Son of God:

> The next day John [the Baptist] saw Jesus coming toward him, and said, "Behold! The Lamb of God who takes away the sin of the world! . . .
> And John bore witness, saying, "I saw the Spirit descending from heaven like a dove, and He remained upon Him. I did not know Him, but He who sent me to baptize with water said to me, 'Upon whom you see the Spirit descending, and remaining on Him, this is He who baptizes with the Holy Spirit.' And I have seen and testified that this is the Son of God."
> Again, the next day, John stood with two of his disciples. And looking at Jesus as He walked, he said, "Behold the Lamb of God!"
>
> John 1:29, 32–36

As we noted earlier, two Persons of the Godhead—the Son and the Spirit—are portrayed in a unique way as figures from the animal kingdom. Jesus is introduced as the Lamb; the Holy Spirit is pictured as descending in the form of a Dove. That is a very beautiful representation of the truth, one that we are highlighting in this book.

The answer to the next question should already be deeply impressed upon your heart by now. But let me ask you again: "What is the Dove looking for?" He is looking for the nature of the Lamb. When He finds the nature of the Lamb in someone, He will not merely descend. He will remain on that person.

Do you remember how I described the nature of the Lamb in chapter 9? I pointed out that in the Bible the Lamb carries certain traits that attract the Holy Spirit—purity, meekness and a life laid down in sacrifice. Do you want to have the Holy Spirit continually with you? Allow Him to have full access to everything in your life, so that He can teach you and transform you into the image of Christ Jesus. He will help you continually to lay down your life for Christ and for His Body. He will convict you when you stray. He will give you joy in purehearted obedience. After a while, you will have matured to the point that you will no longer scare the Dove away.

The Dove on the Veranda

In 1946 I was teaching a children's church in the home we occupied in Jerusalem. Our meetings were held on the first floor in a large entrance hall, and the pulpit was in front of a door in the hall that opened onto a veranda.

On this particular day, I was standing behind the pulpit with my back to the door and veranda, where we had placed a round table with a black tablecloth that was actually an Arab head shawl, a circular piece of cloth.

I was teaching the children about the Holy Spirit that day, and I was telling them that the Holy Spirit is like a dove. "If we want the Dove to stay with us, we have to be very careful we do not say or do anything that would scare Him away."

As I was teaching, I noticed that the children's attention had become riveted on a point behind me. They were absolutely quiet, and their eyes were round and wide open. I was amazed, because I had never received such undivided attention from a group of children.

However, it was not my teaching that had captivated them. Without my knowing it, during my lesson, a beautiful white dove had alighted in the center of that black tablecloth on the table behind me. It was perched there—the white dove standing in absolute contrast to the dark tablecloth. The stock-still children were doing their best to make no movement that might scare the dove away. The Lord had chosen to illustrate my sermon for me. If only we could understand the Holy Spirit as well as those children did that day, we would be more careful in our attitudes toward Him.

23

BEHOLD THE LAMB

In my academic career, I was very successful in my field of study. I had been elected to a fellowship in King's College, Cambridge—one of the youngest men ever to be elected to such a fellowship. I was the senior research student in philosophy at Cambridge for two years in succession. I was a professional philosopher—*philo* meaning "to love" and *sophia* meaning "wisdom." A philosopher is supposed to be someone who loves wisdom, and that applied to me.

As a philosopher, I looked everywhere for the answers to life's problems. When I had looked in the direction of Christianity as it was presented to me in my studies, I simply concluded that Christianity as a religion did not have the answers.

From Greek philosophy, I turned to yoga. Then I turned to all sorts of ridiculous pursuits. Finally, one night in 1941 in an army barracks room sometime about midnight when no one else was awake, I had a personal encounter with the Lord Jesus Christ. Through that encounter, I discovered I had met *the* Answer.

A little later, I read about Jesus Christ in the New Testament: ". . . In whom [Jesus] are hidden all the treasures of wisdom and knowledge" (Colossians 2:3). At that point, I said to myself, *Why should I grub around any longer in the rubbish bins of human wisdom when all the treasures of wisdom and knowledge are hidden in Jesus Christ?* Having been confronted by the cross and having accepted its message, I had to agree with the biblical truth about the wisdom of this world:

> For the message of the cross is foolishness to those who are perishing, but to us who are being saved it is the power of God. For it is written:
> "I will destroy the wisdom of the wise, and bring to nothing the understanding of the prudent."
> Where is the wise? Where is the scribe? Where is the disputer of this age? Has not God made foolish the wisdom of this world?
>
> 1 Corinthians 1:18–20

I made a decision at that time in my life—I decided that the Bible is the book with the Answer, and I wanted to find out all I could about Jesus Christ. I have sometimes been deflected from that resolve since then, but God has always been faithful to put me back on the right track.

Jesus is the Alpha and the Omega, the Beginning and the End, the First and the Last (see Revelation 21:6; 22:13). He is the Author and the Finisher of our faith (see Hebrews 12:2). We are complete in Him. While we may find all sorts of interesting and stimulating theories by looking outside of Jesus Christ for answers to our questions, we will (thinking of Jesus' parable about the prodigal son in Luke 15) find ourselves feeding on husks when we could be feasting on the Father's Bread of Life (see John 6:35).

From the time of my discovery of Christ as the Answer, I have never again bowed to the wisdom of this world. I am no longer impressed by it. Now long lectures in deep theological and philosophical language bore me. The apostle Paul wrote, "For the kingdom of God is not in word but in power" (1 Corinthians 4:20) and that is precisely the way I feel.

Paul practiced what he preached. To the church in Corinth, he wrote:

> And I, brethren, when I came to you, did not come with excellence of speech or of wisdom declaring to you the testimony of God. For I determined not to know anything among you except Jesus Christ and Him crucified.
>
> 1 Corinthians 2:1–2

Paul was a highly educated man. He knew a lot. But he said that he determined "not to know." Perhaps you and I need to determine "not to know"—not to know anything but Jesus and whatever His Holy Spirit shows us. We will need to engage with the people of the world in an intelligent way, but we do not need to follow their direction.

Paul had traveled to Athens, which at the time was the philosophical center of the ancient world. When he spoke to the citizens of Athens, he used their own terminology. He used philosophical language. He even quoted one of their own poets. What were the results of his brilliant approach? In actual fact, they were very meager; only a few people believed.

Paul went on from Athens to Corinth, which was a major port city and a very wicked, licentious city. It would appear that on his way from Athens to Corinth, Paul had made an important decision: "I'm not going to offer them human wisdom. I am not going to know anything among them except Jesus Christ and Him crucified."

Accordingly, Paul told the Corinthian church:

> For you see your calling, brethren, that not many wise according to the flesh, not many mighty, not many noble, are called.
>
> But God has chosen the foolish things of the world to put to shame the wise, and God has chosen the weak things of the world to put to shame the things which are mighty; and the base things of the world and the things which are despised God has chosen, and the things which are not, to bring to nothing the things that are, that no flesh should glory in His presence.
>
> 1 Corinthians 1:26–29

These verses tell us that God has made His choice: "God has chosen." He is not *preparing* to choose; He has already made His decision—and none of us can persuade God to change His mind. God has chosen the weak things to confound the mighty; the foolish things to confound the wise; the base things to confound that which is honorable.

What a strange list. Which category are you in? Do you consider yourself dignified, respectable and intelligent? Surprisingly, if that is how you regard yourself, God cannot use you, because you are outside the field of His choice.

In chapter 11, we recognized that there are times when God calls us to be weak or foolish. In fact, He may send a "thorn in the flesh" to you and me as he did with Paul, to keep us humble and reliant on Him. We ought to welcome such humbling circumstances. Growing into the nature of the Lamb involves being prepared to look weak or foolish, and if we are not prepared for that possibility, there will be

215

a definite limit to how fully the Holy Spirit will be able to use us.

Paul's first letter to the Corinthians dwells consistently on the theme of being foolish in order to be used by God. His second letter to them focuses attention on being weak in order to be used by God.

Taken together, his instructions help us better understand how the way of the Lamb is a way of humility, weakness and even foolishness:

> For Jews request a sign, and Greeks seek after wisdom; but we preach Christ crucified, to the Jews a stumbling block and to the Greeks foolishness, but to those who are called, both Jews and Greeks, Christ the power of God and the wisdom of God. Because the foolishness of God is wiser than men, and the weakness of God is stronger than men.
>
> 1 Corinthians 1:22–25

> Let no one deceive himself. If anyone among you seems to be wise in this age, let him become a fool that he may become wise. For the wisdom of this world is foolishness with God. For it is written, "He catches the wise in their own craftiness"; and again, "The Lord knows the thoughts of the wise, that they are futile." Therefore let no one boast in men. For all things are yours: whether Paul or Apollos or Cephas, or the world or life or death, or things present or things to come— all are yours. And you are Christ's, and Christ is God's.
>
> 1 Corinthians 3:18–23

How true it is that the Lord "knows the thoughts of the wise, that they are futile"! Philosophy in the Western world has a history of about 2,500 years, starting about the fifth century before Christ. So far, in all that time, philosophers have not yet even decided on the questions they are trying to resolve, much less resolve any of them. It seems that God is right!

I always get nervous when I hear contemporary preachers quoting psychiatrists and experts. Now, I believe psychiatrists provide a wonderful service. But the Word of God does not need to be supported by psychiatry or psychology. It stands on its own. Propping up the Word of God with human wisdom opens a door that can undermine faith. Building our faith on human wisdom provides a very insubstantial foundation—one that will likely shift in the next generation. We can do better than that.

We can fully depend upon the Holy Spirit to lead us into all truth. That is why one of His names is the Helper (see John 14:26; 15:26; 16:7). Without the Helper, we remain in ignorance: "And if anyone thinks that he knows anything, he knows nothing yet as he ought to know" (1 Corinthians 8:2).

"Humble yourselves under the mighty hand of God, that He may exalt you in due time" (1 Peter 5:6). Let us turn our attention, with the help of the Dove, to the nature of the Lamb, so we will be able to come to a place of rest and revelation at the feet of Jesus.

Beholding the Lamb

Years ago, I was the speaker at a conference with the theme "Behold the Lamb!" At one point, I suggested that we should stop everything for a little while and simply behold the Lamb, adoring our Savior, Jesus Christ. This is what my dear, departed friend Johannes Facius used to call "wasting time on Jesus."

The picture that comes to mind is of Mary of Bethany, who sat at the feet of Jesus and listened to His words. When her busy sister, Martha, became perturbed and asked Jesus to make Mary help her, Jesus said, "Mary has chosen that good part, which will not be taken away from her" (Luke 10:42).

Sometime later when they were eating together in the house of Simon the leper, many believe it was Mary who came in holding the most expensive item she owned—an alabaster jar of ointment, which was worth nearly a year's wages. Did Mary bring it to Jesus as a gift? Yes and no. She broke the vessel (which was the only way to get the ointment out) and poured the ointment on Jesus' head (see Mark 14:4–9).

Some of the disciples were indignant, saying, "Why was this fragrant oil wasted? For it might have been sold for more than three hundred denarii and given to the poor" (vv. 4–5). But Jesus commended the woman, and then He reminded them that they would have the poor with them always, but He would not be with them much longer.

Then Jesus said, "She has done what she could. She has come beforehand to anoint My body for burial" (v. 8). The Jewish people always anointed a body before it was buried. Mary was the only one who did it for Jesus. Later on (see Mark 16:1), when the other women came early to the tomb with ointment and spices to anoint the body of Jesus, they were too late—He had already risen!

Mary must have known ahead of time. It is my personal belief that she got that revelation while sitting at the feet of Jesus. Revelation comes from being in the presence of the Lord.

You and I can develop some good plans and ideas in our determination to follow the Lord, and we can carry them out. However, the only work that has any value is whatever God initiates. And the best place to find out what God is initiating is at the feet of Jesus.

Ruth and I have learned this, at least in a measure. Unless we are committed to another engagement, we have dedicated every Wednesday to waiting upon the Lord. We used to have a long prayer list, and it was a very good prayer list. But waiting on the Lord does not require a prayer list. In fact, you need no agenda, and you do not want to set any time limit.

The Lord will give you *His* agenda, and it will be good to bear in mind that you cannot rush God. The waiting period may only be a matter of minutes, or it could be a matter of hours. I recommend that you take a little sip of the wine of waiting; maybe you will develop a taste for it.

Come to Him Now

Now, my dear reader, it may be that you feel at this point in your life that you are not really as committed to the Lord Jesus as you want to be. You may feel as if you are not following the Lamb in the way I have described. Perhaps you are not sure that the qualities of your nature will attract the Dove to descend and remain upon you. Possibly you do not feel totally called, chosen and faithful.

Have factors such as these convinced you that you do not want to continue in your present condition? Even such a realization reveals the operation of the Word and the Spirit together. Remember, whenever the Word and the Spirit of God are united in our experience, the total creative power of God is available to us. You can count on it being true for you.

As the Bible says, "Consider your ways" (Haggai 1:7). Ask yourself: "Have I committed myself without reservation to the Lordship of Jesus Christ? Am I willing to do whatever He leads me to do? How am I cultivating and manifesting the nature of the Lamb? Is the Dove remaining on me?"

If you long for a big change, or if you simply want to refresh your relationship with the Lamb and the Dove, you can pray this prayer right now:

Lord Jesus,

I want to refresh my commitment to You. I want to humble myself before You, to receive Your forgiveness, and to walk from this day forward in the empowerment that comes from Your Holy Spirit. I want to lay down my life daily for You, walking in purity and meekness, manifesting the nature of the Lamb.

May the Dove (Your Holy Spirit) bring forth in me the nature of the Lamb (Jesus Christ, the Messiah) so that I may be able to stand strong and victorious in the challenging days now and yet to come, fully obeying You and faithfully serving You. Amen.

Derek Prince (1915–2003) was born in India of British parents. He was educated as a scholar of Greek and Latin at Eton College and Cambridge University, England, where he held a fellowship in ancient and modern philosophy at King's College. He also studied several modern languages, including Hebrew and Aramaic, at Cambridge University and the Hebrew University in Jerusalem.

While serving with the British Army in World War II, Derek began to study the Bible and experienced a life-changing encounter with Jesus Christ. Out of that encounter he formed two conclusions: first, that Jesus Christ is alive; and second, that the Bible is a true, relevant, up-to-date book. These conclusions altered the course of his life, which he then devoted to studying and teaching the Bible.

People from all racial and religious backgrounds find his teaching relevant and helpful because of its nondenominational, nonsectarian approach. His teaching can be found in more than eighty books, six hundred audio recordings and one hundred video resources, many of which have been translated into more than a hundred languages. His daily radio broadcast, *Keys to Successful Living*, continues to touch lives around the world and has been translated into Arabic, Chinese, Croatian, German, Malagasy, Mongolian, Russian, Samoan, Spanish and Tongan.

For more information on Derek Prince and the many teaching resources available, please contact:

Derek Prince Ministries International
P.O. Box 19501
Charlotte, NC 28219-9501
(704) 357-3556
derekprince.org

More from Derek Prince

What are demons, and how do they gain entry into people's lives? Derek Prince addresses the fears and misconceptions associated with demons and encourages believers to become equipped and take action against these evil beings. He offers solid advice on how to receive and minister deliverance—and how to remain free.

They Shall Expel Demons

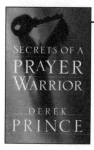

Beloved author Derek Prince shows readers the secret to leading a dynamic prayer life, how to receive what they ask for, and how to align themselves with the heart of God. This book includes practical strategies such as fasting, biblical study, discipline and consistency, and is illustrated by powerful testimonies.

Secrets of a Prayer Warrior

 Stay up to date on your favorite books and authors with our free e-newsletters. Sign up today at chosenbooks.com.

 facebook.com/chosenbooks

 @Chosen_Books

 @chosen_books